FREE TO PRAY — FREE TO LOVE

Father Max Oliva,

a Jesuit priest living in San Diego, California, has been conducting retreats, seminars, and workshops on spirituality and prayer since 1974. He has given retreats throughout the U.S., in Ireland, and in South Africa, and also serves part-time in a mission in Tijuana, Mexico. He is also the author of *Praying the Beatitudes*.

FREE TO PRAY — FREE TO LOVE

Growing in Prayer & Compassion

MAX OLIVA, S.J.

VERITAS

Unless noted otherwise, the Bible text used in this book is from the *Today's English Version*, copyright © American Bible Society, 1976, 1992. Used by permission.

Excerpts from *Open Mind, Open Heart* copyright 1991 by Thomas Keating are used by permission of Element Books. All rights reserved.

Excerpt from *Prayers for the Domestic Church* copyright 1979 by Edward Hays are used by permission of Forest of Peace Books. All rights reserved.

Excerpts from *The Marriage of East and West* copyright 1982 by Bede Griffiths are used by permission of Templegate Publishers. All rights reserved.

Excerpts from *New Seeds of Contemplation* by Thomas Merton copyright © 1961 by The Abbey of Gethsemani, Inc. Reprinted by permission of New Directions Publishing Corp.

Excerpts from *How Can I Help?* by Ram Dass and Paul Gorman, copyright © 1985 by Ram Dass and Paul Gorman. Reprinted by permission of Alfred A. Knopf, Inc.

Published in Ireland by Veritas Publications, 7-8 Lower Abbey Street, Dublin, Ireland.

ISBN: 1 85390 275 6

Cover photograph by John J. Morgan, Jr.

Cover and text design by Katherine Robinson Coleman

Printed and bound in the United States of America.

Dedication

In memory of my father.

To those Jesuits who have been my mentors,
with special thanks to Fathers Francis Silva,
Harry Corcoran, Dick Vaughan, Dan O'Hanlon,
and Herbert Dargan.

And to the many people I have met on retreats,
whose deep faith and searching hearts have
enriched my own journey of faith.

Acknowledgments

I give thanks to God for the many people who have contributed to the writing of this book:

My community in San Diego, especially Dave and Lucy Hokanson and their family, Carl and Mimi Smith, Gary and Bobbie Glasheen, Candy Bojorquez, Augustinians Dick Hardick, Walt Vogel, Jim Mott, Harry Neely, and Mike Harkay, the Friday morning men's Cursillo group, and Sister Maggie Yee for their loving support. Thanks as well to the priests of St. Michael's Parish—Mel Collier, Romi Supnet, and Matt Spahr—and the staff at St. Michael's; it was here that I lived when I wrote the book.

The parishioners of Nuestra Señora de la Esperanza Church, in Tijuana, Mexico, where I have served for seven years in a part-time capacity. Their trust in God while in difficult economic circumstances is a constant inspiration to me.

Father Bob Fabing, my brother Jesuit, for twenty-five years of friendship and for the varied insights into the spiritual life that I have gained from our conversations.

Sister Theresa McGrath, C.C.V.I., for her friendship and for her helpful comments on the manuscript.

Sister Imelda Phelan, C.S.B., for her friendship and encouragement.

Special thanks to three Jesuit spiritual guides in my journey: Carroll O'Sullivan, who helped me to believe in God's unconditional love; Joe Carroll, who assisted me in discovering my true, affective self; and Frank Houdek, who was my retreat director when I first discovered the Freedom-Prayer.

Irish soul friends Monica Byrne, Margaret Mooney, and Myles O'Reilly, S.J., whose inquiring minds and courage in the quest for union with God have pushed me further than I thought it possible to go.

Sister Paula Thompson, O.S.B., who introduced me to the writings of Beatrice Bruteau, an American spiritual writer. And, to Ms. Bruteau for her clarity of insight that has been of great assistance in understanding my inner life.

Sisters Electa Hevener and Joanna Gombold, O.C.D., for their conscientious proofreading and typing. And, to Mary Creagh for her patient preparation of the manuscript for publication.

Fathers Wilkie Au and Tom Hand, S.J., for their careful reading of the manuscript and for their helpful critique.

Bob Hamma, my excellent editor at Ave Maria Press, for his encouragement and for his gentle manner in suggesting changes in the text.

And finally, to my siblings, Marcia, Kathy, Marilyn, and Paul. Though we follow different paths, we are close in spirit, able to learn from one another how to become more free and more loving.

Contents

Introduction

This book is about freedom in the spiritual journey, a freedom that is based on the love of God and expresses itself in love for all that God has created.

As a Jesuit I have been profoundly influenced by the charism of St. Ignatius of Loyola, founder of the Society of Jesus. In his *Spiritual Exercises*, a classic retreat manual, the opening meditation is called "The First Principle and Foundation." A partial reading, in modern translation, is:

> The goal of our life is to live with God forever. God gave us life because God loves us. Our own response of love allows God's life to flow into us without limit.
>
> All the things in this world are gifts of God, presented to us so that we can know God more easily and make a return of love more readily.
>
> As a result, we appreciate and use all these gifts of God insofar as they help us develop as loving persons. But if any of these gifts becomes the center of our lives, they displace God and so hinder our growth towards our goal.
>
> Our only desire and our one choice should be this: I want and I choose what better leads to God's deepening of life within me.[1]

The key theme of this meditation is interior freedom. We are to be detached from all created things, not in an aloof or disinterested way but in balance, that is, at peace in whatever God asks of us in the circumstances of our life. Everything has the potential of calling forth in us a deeper response to God.

It is an underlying supposition of this book that each of us is called to be free. Each of us is invited to be a mystic. The purpose of this book is to show, in a variety of ways, how God leads us to wholeness and holiness. To assist us in this journey, I share significant parts of my own story. It is my hope that this will help the reader to reflect on her or his own experience of God. In addition, I make liberal use of the Bible, other spiritual writers, and authors from other disciplines. Throughout the book different forms of prayer are proposed while at the same time prayer methods are presented so that the reader may practice an exercise while reading a particular chapter.

The foundation for this journey of freedom is the unconditional love of God. In the first chapter we consider this fundamental article of our faith as the basis of our personal identity and we look at some of the resistances we have to accepting God's everlasting love.

Our realization of God's love for us enables us to look at those parts of our personality that enslave us. In chapter two I share a form of prayer that has come out of my own experience. I call it "freedom-prayer." This method of prayer offers a chance for deliverance from many obstacles within ourselves that imprison our love. On our pilgrimage to union with God we are guided along many avenues of prayer. In chapter three we review four prayer forms: meditation on the scriptures, prayer of the imagination, centering prayer, and quiet prayer.

Various changes in consciousness happen in us as we progress in the spiritual journey. In chapters four and five we reflect on such transformations as the unloading of the unconscious, living in the present moment, Christ-consciousness, and the importance of intuition in our life of prayer. Chapter six takes us into a consideration of the dark nights of sense and of the spirit.

Prayer and changes in consciousness do not take us away from concern for what is happening in the world, rather they lead us to a deeper embrace of it. Chapter seven stretches our inner freedom as we ponder the call to compassion and social justice, two important ways we live out our love for others. In this context we also consider the role of intuition in our caring for the wounded in society.

In recent years, many of us have heard the cries of our anguished planet, and we have become saddened by the extent of damage that has been done to it. Chapter eight takes us into compassion for the earth, extending our love to all of creation. As we seek to develop an eco-spirituality to counter eco-destruction, we reflect on the example of St. Francis of Assisi, heavenly patron of ecology. We look back into our own history to discover the seeds of our concern for creation. We then consider what responses we might make as disciples of the One who created all that exists.

In the final chapter we return to the theme of interior freedom by reflecting on Thomas Merton's teaching on the true self—the self in Christ grounded in the love of God. This is the journey we are on, to realize more and more our true self.

The route to union with God in the freedom of love is not always a clear one. It is hoped that, by sharing significant episodes from my own journey and by high-lighting the insights of many of the authors who have helped me to understand my own experiences, the reader may more easily discover God's presence in her or his life.

One

The Unconditional Love of God

> [My child,] keep your self-respect, but remain modest. Value yourself at your true worth. There is no excuse for a person to run [him/herself] down. No one respects a person who has no respect for [him/herself.]
>
> —*Sirach 10:28-29*

Perhaps the most elusive element in a person's spiritual life is the conviction that he or she is loved, and loved unconditionally, by God. We daily meet many temptations against this truth. Some come from within ourselves, while others find their source in the values of society. Thomas Merton, in his book *New Seeds of Contemplation*, wrote: "The root of Christian love is not the will to love, but the faith that one is loved. The faith that one is loved by God."[1]

God's love is *the* foundation of our life. Upon it rests our ultimate identity, our integrity, our hope. It is the good news that sets us free. As one author states it, "Liberation is the experience by which a person realizes in a personal way that he/she is loved and is enabled to act out of this realization."[2]

This is not, however, what society tells us about identity. How much money we make, the kind of neighborhood we live in, the number of prized possessions we have, the exclusive clubs we belong to, the designer fashions we wear, the important people we know—these are the measures society would have us use for our self-worth and the worth of others.

The kind of self-valuing that the gospel teaches is only reached by continual conversion. We need to experience a conversion in regard to ourselves based on the unconditional love of God. Perhaps a story from my own life will clarify this process of conversion.

I joined the Jesuit Order at the age of twenty-four. At the time, I was a salesman for a food cannery. My prospects were good. I had Oregon, Washington, and Western Canada for a territory. An expense account enabled me to stay at the best hotels when I went on sales trips. At home, I drove a fancy sports car. I prided myself on the beauty of the women I went out with. My lifestyle was that of a young bachelor with money to spend.

Into the midst of this way of life came the quite unexpected realization that deep down I wanted to be a priest! Consequently, in the short span of a month, I went from the business world to the Jesuit novitiate, where I found myself in the company of men five and six years younger. In the early days of the novitiate, I experienced feelings of what might be called self-deprecation. For reasons I could not fathom at the time, I would occasionally feel down about myself. I brought this account of my feelings to my spiritual director who suggested I say a particular phrase every time these negative emotions appeared: "God loves me and nothing else matters." He advised me to repeat this as needed, even though I would not believe it at first. In addition, he encouraged me to read passages from the Bible highlighting God's love. Subsequently, we met periodically to reflect on what was happening in me.

It was during the novitiate that I came to realize that I had a very poor self-image. Some causes for this came to mind: guilt for past mistakes and an inferiority complex that had its origins in my childhood. In order to compensate for my lack of self-worth, I had, unconsciously, filled the hole in my psyche with possessions. I imagined myself to be worthwhile because of the kind of car I owned, the important people I knew, my success as a salesman, and the lifestyle I led. It gradually became clear, as I prayed and reflected on this, that I had been defining my self by externals, by the things outside me. In the novitiate, finding myself without these entities, I came face to face with the naked truth of my identity.

Anyone can come to a similar awareness of his or her basic identity. The unexpected loss of one's job, retirement, a serious physical disability that limits one's capacity for work, the "empty-nest" syndrome, the death of a loved one, and so forth, can occasion a new look at one's true identity. Being caught in such a dilemma can lead to discouragement and even despair, or can point the way to a deeper conversion.

Conversion is what happened to me. The more I said the words, "God loves me and nothing else matters," the more I came to believe in God's love for me. At the time, I was surrounded by loving people; I experienced God loving me through them. Certain passages from the Bible started to make sense as I applied them to myself—Isaiah 43:4, for example: "You are precious in my eyes and glorious, and … I love you" (*NAB*); and, "I give you thanks that I am fearfully, wonderfully made" (Psalm 139:14, *NAB*); and, "The mountains and hills may crumble, but my love for you will never end; I will keep forever my promise of peace. So says the LORD who loves you" (Isaiah 54:10). And, from the First Letter of John: "This is what love is: it is not that we have loved God, but that [God] loved us and sent [the] Son to be the means by which our sins are forgiven" (4:10). Even my focus on the passion of Christ changed. Whereas before I had concentrated on my sins as putting Christ on the cross, I now look at the cross as his supreme gift of love for me and for all people.

Beatrice Bruteau, in an excellent article called "Prayer and Identity," suggests that the work of prayer is to transform our sense of identity.[3] Prayer helps us to clarify who we are to ourselves, beyond the roles we play, beyond what *describes* us, to a deeper dimension of selfhood. We tend, she points out, to *identify* with what describes us: "I am a school principal," "I make this amount in salary," "I drive a Mercedes," "I have a Ph.D. in Physics," "I belong to the Country Club," and so on. Each may be true, but only as descriptions. They are not *me*. A marvelous illustration of this comes from the book, *How Can I Help?* The authors recount the following story by a young doctor:

> As an intern, part of my work was to travel around in teams, examining patients. I would notice their look as we entered. Intimidated, apprehensive, feeling like case studies of various illnesses. I hated that. But I was an intern.
>
> I remember one guy distinctly, however, who was altogether different. I think this guy changed my life. He was a black man in his sixties—very cute, very mischievous, and very sick.
>
> What brought us repeatedly to him was the utter complexity of his illness, condition on top of condition, and the mystery of why he was still here at all.
>
> I had the feeling he could see right through us. He'd say, "Hey, boys!" when we'd come in— the way you might when a gang of ten-year-olds come barging into a house for a snack in the middle of an intense game outside. He was so pleased, and so amused. It made some people nervous. I was intrigued. But for some weeks, I never had a chance to be alone with him.
>
> Now and then he'd get into very serious trouble, and he'd be moved into intensive care. Then he'd rally, to everyone's amazement, and he'd say, "You boys here again?"—pretending to be surprised that *we* were still around.
>
> One night there was an emergency, and I took the initiative and went to see him alone. He looked pretty bad. But he came alert a few seconds after I entered. He gave me a grin and said, "Well … " sort of like he'd expected me. Like he'd known how much I'd come to love him. That happens in hospi-

tals. I imagined I looked a little surprised at the "Well ... " but we just laughed a minute, and I stood there just so taken by who he was. And then he hit me with a single remark, half a question and half a ... something else.

"Who you?" he said, sort of smiling. Just that. "Who you?"

I started to say, "Well, I'm Doctor ...." And then I just stopped cold. It's hard to describe. I just sort of went out. What happened was that all kinds of answers to his question started to go through my head. They all seemed true, but they all seemed less than true. "Yeah, I'm this or that ... and also ... but not just ... and that's not the whole picture, the whole picture is ... " The thought process went something like that. Nothing remotely like that had ever happened to me. But I remember feeling elated.

It must have shown, because he gave me this big grin and said, "Nice to meet you." His timing killed me.

We talked for five minutes about this and that—nothing in particular; children, I think. At the end, I ventured to say, "Is there anything I can do for you?" He said, "No, I'm just fine. Thanks very much ... Doctor ...?" And he paused for the name, and I gave it to him this time, and he grinned at me again, really he did. And that was it. He died a few days later. And I carry him around today. I think of him now and again in the midst of my rounds. A particular patient brings him back. "Who you?" For years, I'd trained to be a physician, and I almost got lost in it. This man took away my degree, and then gave it back to me with "And also? ... and also ... and also?" scribbled across. I'll never forget that.[4]

"Who you?" helps us to get to the root of our identity.

Resistance to God's Unconditional Love

In addition to an obsession with things as a way of shoring up a shaky self-image, there are other ways we can be blind to God's love.

A few years ago, while giving an eight-day directed retreat (in which the retreatant meets with a director once a day to discern how best to pray), I met someone with an exaggerated feeling of unworthiness. Briefly, this is the belief that one is nothing and no good. Words like, "I should" and "I ought" flow freely from such a person. This negative way of thinking about oneself leads to a false understanding of humility. Humility is truth and the truth is "I am fearfully, wonderfully made" (Psalm 139:14, *NAB*). I am "limited, yet loved; sinful, yet valued." Or, in the words of Julian of Norwich, "endlessly treasured." Self-esteem is genuine pride, to be humble you have to have some confidence in yourself. In the Book of Sirach we are instructed, "[My child,] keep your self-respect, but remain modest. Value yourself at your true worth" (Sirach 10:28).

Having self-esteem does not mean that I am perfect nor that I have no more growing to do. It does mean that I acknowledge the good I do, the talents I have, and the beauty that exists in my particular personality. Sister Francis Brennan, an eighty-year-old inspiration on self-affirmation, shared with me the following list of positive statements that she says out loud each morning:

> Because you love me, Father, I am able to love myself unconditionally just the way I am.
>
> I never devalue myself through destructive self-criticism.
>
> I have unconditional warm regard for all persons at all times.
>
> I am easily able to relax at any time and every day; through each affirmation I grow healthier in body, mind, and spirit.

I am completely self-determined, inner guided by the Holy Spirit, and I allow others the same right.

I refuse to give control to any person, circumstance, or thing to annoy or upset me.

Happiness and joy are my normal states of mind. I have a wonderful sense of humor, and I enjoy a good laugh every day.[5]

A second misconception, a form of blindness to the unconditional quality of God's love, is that love must be earned. If I work really hard or do these good deeds, then God will love me. Of course, this is how we often experience love from other human beings. Parents naturally reward their children when they are good and punish them when they are bad. However, when the punishment is perceived by the child as a withholding of love, or when love is clearly given only as reward—for cleaning one's room, studying hard, working for spending money, mowing the lawn, and so forth—the child grows up with an understanding of love as conditional. Such a child will transfer this experience of love from parent to God, imaging God as one who loves for what and how much is done, and how well it is done. We do not have to search far in the scriptures to find the error in this kind of reasoning:

This is what love is: it is not that we have loved God, but that [God] loved us.... We love because God first loved us (1 John 4:10, 19).

It is interesting to note that God showed love for Jesus *before* Jesus' public life, that is, before he went about doing good works. Gerard Fourez states it quite well: "The liberation, the realization of the Good News, is the awareness that one is loved independently of whatever one does."[6] As one retreatant expressed his view of God's love: "I can't earn it, and I can't lose it!" Saint Augustine put it this way: "God loves each one of us as if there were one of us."

Those who struggle with this kind of blindness to God's love without conditions can find it helpful to recall experiences of being loved where there were no conditions. In my life, this has been through the love of children. My ministry includes serving in a small, mission parish in Tijuana, Mexico. The children there are spontaneous in their affection, unguarded and uncalculating. It is in their love that I have had a glimpse of what God's love must be like.

I recall a retreatant who complained he could not find value in himself outside of his ministry. He asked God to free him from this bind. During one of his prayer periods, he was led to see himself as a child, sitting on Jesus' lap, being loved. The Lord was loving him before he was old enough to work. This was a tremendously freeing experience for him, affecting how he valued himself from then on.

A third obstacle to fully appreciating the love of God is the inability to forgive ourselves for something we have done wrong. Fr. George Auger explains:

> We say to ourselves, "I, of all people, should be beyond the weakness I experience." Thinking this, and similar thoughts, we become impatient with ourselves and even perhaps discouraged. We find it impossible to love ourselves in our weakness. We cannot love ourselves as God loves us.[7]

He recalls how St. Thérèse of Lisieux learned to love herself, in her weakness, when she was a young girl. She said:

> I know for certain that even if I had on my conscience all the sins that can be committed, I would not become discouraged. I would joyfully cast myself in the arms of Jesus. I know how he cherishes the prodigal child who returns to him.[8]

We are reminded of the experience of Julian of Norwich. God revealed to her the pain that sin causes and warned her that she, too, would fail in love. At the same time, God comforted her in her distress at hearing this message by promising to keep her secure. God told her, "All shall be well, and all shall be well, and all manner of things shall be well."[9] God loved her, and us, not in spite of her weakness, but because of it. Her emphasis is more on the love and mercy of God than on her imperfections. That is the secret! We are to focus, not on our wrongdoing, but on the compassion of our God.

Here is a prayer for granting forgiveness to oneself:

My God, You who perpetually pardon
    all who are sincere in their sorrow,
    help me as I seek to forgive myself.
I realize, my Lord, that unless I can forgive myself
    I cannot fully forgive those who have offended me.
Humble my heart
    so that I can embrace all that is hidden within me.

You, Lord of Creation,
    have divided time into day and night.
My life is likewise divided
    between light and darkness,
    good and bad.
When these dark, negative needs are excessive
    and out of balance with the positive,
    they become destructive to others,
    and to myself as well.

I forgive myself for becoming impatient
    because I was too busy, too particular, or in a hurry.
I forgive myself for this failing
    as I forgive others who are impatient, too.
I forgive myself for making mistakes,
    for being too quick to act or to speak,
    for not taking time to think;
I forgive myself as well as others
    who make their own mistakes.
I forgive myself for being stupid in sinning, for
    falling into the same errors which injure others and
    myself.
I forgive myself for those small sins
    that irritate others and cause me shame.
For a smallness of mind in my thoughts,
    for a narrowness of heart in my actions,

I forgive myself
and forgive others who act and think as I do.

Compassionate Lord, I know how I sin most easily;
help me to understand and to correct this failing.

A pause for silent reflection may be used here.

I grant myself pardon and forgiveness
so that my darkness may fuel the goodness within me,
a goodness which you, my God,
have placed in great deposit within me.

Amen.[10]

In offering this prayer, we rely on the compassionate power of God to heal us of the hardness of heart we have toward ourself. It is a prayer for the grace to know we are limited yet loved.

In retreats, I often use a simple prayer of the presence of Christ, similar to the one that St. Teresa of Avila taught her sisters. I ask retreatants to:

Close your eyes.

Take a couple of deep breaths.

Relax.

Now, imagine you have Jesus in front of you.

He is looking at you.

Notice him looking at you.

Listen to him as he tells you how much he loves you.

If you find yourself feeling uncomfortable, blocking this gift of love in any way, ask Jesus to free you of this obstacle.

Rest in his love.

Now, spend a few moments thanking Jesus, in your heart, for his great love.

Open your eyes when you feel ready to do so.[11]

Sometimes a crisis, or trauma, or some suffering causes us to question the love of God. We say, "If God loves me, why did this happen?" Our faith can be severely tested when someone close to us dies, when we suffer unemployment or face bankruptcy, or when a debilitating accident happens to us. A couple of years ago, I experienced three significant losses in the space of two months: my father died, just short of his eightieth birthday; my brother and sisters and I decided to sell the family home (very traumatic for me as I do not have my own property); and, due to a change of pastors at the parish where I had been in residence for three good years, I had to find another living situation.

In the midst of dealing with the grief associated with these three losses, and the feelings of insecurity that came with not knowing where I would live, a friend of mine gave me a book called, *The Joy of Full Surrender*, by Jean-Pierre de Caussade. At the time when my spirits were at their lowest, I read these words from his book, "We are troubled and disturbed, yet nevertheless in our depths we have some unseen anchor that keeps us clinging to God."[12] That "unseen anchor" of faith kept me secure even though my spirit was in darkness and God seemed very far away. And, even though I could not *feel* God's love, I knew, by the very words I read, that God was close at hand. On the previous page of the book, Father de Caussade had written:

> To live by faith is to live by joy, confidence, and certainty about all that has to be done or suffered at each moment by God's will. It is in order to animate and to maintain this life of faith that God allows us to be plunged into and carried away by the rough waters of numerous pains, troubles, difficulties, weaknesses and defeats. For it requires faith to find God in all these.[13]

Thomas Keating recounts an interesting interpretation, given by the early fathers of the church, of this verse of the Song of Songs, "O that his left hand were under my head and that his right hand embraced me" (Song 2:6):

God embraces us with both arms. With the left God humbles and corrects us; with the right God lifts us up and consoles us with the assurance of being loved. If you want to be fully embraced by the Lord, you have to accept both arms: the one that allows suffering for the sake of purification and the one that brings the joy of union. When you feel physical pain or when psychological struggles are persecuting you, you should think that God is hugging you extra tightly.[14]

Or, listen to the poetic way that Thomas Merton describes the all encompassing nature of God's love:

It is God's love that warms me in the sun and God's love that sends the cold rain. It is God's love that feeds me also by hunger and fasting. It is the love of God that sends the winter days when I am cold and sick, and the hot summer when I labor and my clothes are full of sweat: but it is God who breathes on me with light winds off the river and in the breezes out of the wood.[15]

There are people so preoccupied by an exalted opinion of themselves—what the Greeks called *hubris* or arrogance—that they are blind to the truth of their dependence for life and sustenance on someone greater than themselves. Steeped in self-sufficiency, they have neither faith in, nor fear of, God. One thinks of the dictator who rules his constituency by tyranny, of the business executive whose god is money, of the egotist who judges himself as superior to everyone else, or of the church or government leader who has power as her deity. This kind of pride is a firm barrier to realizing God's love.

It is true that "pride goes before the fall," but my experience of giving retreats has shown me that most of us struggle with self-acceptance more than with an overwhelming sense of self. Wilkie Au states it well: "We are constantly tempted with self-rejection. Inner voices disturb our peace and tell us we are not good-looking enough, not rich enough, not talented enough."[16] I would add, "not dedicated enough, not doing enough." Kathleen Fischer, in her excellent book *Women at the Well*, writes about the experience of women as being "conditioned to see themselves as inferior."[17] Writing about discernment, she states:

> Women do not typically need to hear the constant references to the dangers of self-love, selfishness, and self-centeredness which punctuate most discussions of discernment. In my experience, women do not usually choose the path of death rather than life because of self-love. Rather, as so much feminist literature makes clear, their choices go wrong because of an inability to love self well.[18]

It is not only women who face "not loving themselves well." People who are discriminated against, put down, thought of as inferior—whether because of the color of their skin, their mother language, their culture, or their sexual orientation—are caught in the same trap. In South Africa, for example, there is still a form of discrimination against people of color who are believed to be less developed, less civilized, unintelligent, slow thinkers, irresponsible, and lazy. If someone is told this enough, he or she will internalize the views of the other, ending up in a posture of self-hatred. It takes time, a lot of positive affirmation, and the grace of God to reverse such a negative way of thinking about oneself.

The Fullness of Love

Attainment of the fullness of love—the realization of one's own value as seen through the eyes of God—is a life-long project. There is need for conversion, not once but many times. This is so because, as we have seen, there are so many temptations against having God's love as the center of our life. There are so many "idols" that keep getting in the way. At the beginning of this chapter, I related my basic conversion experience. I was led to accept

God's unconditional love as the foundation of my identity. Fourteen years later I was to have another startling revelation. It took place at Emerald Bay, Lake Tahoe, in Northern California. It was a beautiful day, not a cloud in the sky. I was sitting on the mountainside, about one hundred feet above the lake. Close by, a waterfall tumbled down the mountain toward the lake below. Majestic pine trees rose up behind me, as did the jagged peaks of the mountains. Similar trees lined the lakeshore. Emerald Bay, with its tiny island in view, lay before me like a jewel. It was breathtaking. I felt so grateful to God for this marvelous gift of creation. In the midst of my reverie, this thought came to my consciousness: "Yes, this is beautiful, but in my eyes you are more beautiful." I was overwhelmed. Tears came to my eyes, tears of joy and gratitude. Deep down within myself I realized anew what it means to be made in the image and likeness of God. I was converted to a more profound appreciation of myself, to a fuller love of myself.

To truly know ourselves, we must be consciously aware of our inner glory (see Psalm 8:5-6), and to come to that we need to ask God for help. We must pray. The words God spoke to Jesus after he was baptized, "This is my beloved Son. My favor rests on him" (Matthew 3:17, *NAB*), are addressed to us too. "You are my beloved daughter/son. My favor rests on you." It is valuable in our spiritual journey periodically to reflect on our experiences of God's love: a special moment of grace, the love of a good friend, the birth of a baby, a trial miraculously passed through, any experience where we knew ourselves as loved just as we are. St. John wrote, "We ourselves know and believe the love which God has for us" (1 John 4:16). A good question to reflect on is: How have I come to know and to believe in the love God has for me?

St. Ignatius of Loyola, the founder of the Jesuits, wrote this reflection on God:

God's love shines down on me
Like the rays from the sun....

Just as I see the sun in its rays,
so God pours forth himself
in all the gifts which he showers upon me.[19]

A help to attaining the fullness of love is to let God speak to us, personally, in the words of the scriptures. For example, when hearing the following passage from the prophet Isaiah, as he relates the sentiment of God, we can substitute our own name for that of Israel:

Israel, the LORD who created you says,
"Do not be afraid—I will save you.
I have called you by name—you are mine.
When you pass through deep waters,
I will be with you....
When you pass through fire, you will
not be burned ... (Isaiah 43:1-2).

"Deep waters" and "fire" are symbolic of the personal trials we go through. God is with us in every crisis. Should we question God's presence in difficult times, we can draw consolation from these words from the book of Isaiah:

But the people of Jerusalem said,
"The LORD has abandoned us!
[The Lord] has forgotten us."
So the LORD answers,
"Can a woman forget her own baby
and not love the child she bore?
Even if a mother should forget her child,
I will never forget you. ...

I have written your name on the
palms of my hands" (Isaiah 49:14-16).

One of the most caring passages of the whole Bible is Psalm 23. Here is a beautiful Native American version of it:

The Great Father above a Shepherd Chief is.
I am His and with Him I want not.
He throws out to me a rope

and the name of the rope is love
and He draws me to where the grass is green
and the water is not dangerous,
and I eat and lie down and am satisfied.
Sometimes my heart is very weak and falls down
but He lifts me up again and draws me into a
    good road.
His name is Wonderful.

Sometime, it may be very soon, it may be a
    long long time,
He will draw me into a valley.
It is dark there, but I'll be afraid not,
for it is between those mountains
that the Shepherd Chief will meet me
and the hunger that I have in my heart all
    through life
will be satisfied.

Sometimes He makes the love rope into a whip,
but afterwards He gives me a staff to lean upon.
He spreads a table before me with all kinds
    of foods.
He puts His hand upon my head and all the "tired"
    is gone.
My cup He fills till it runs over.
What I tell is true.
I lie not.
These roads that are "away ahead" will stay
    with me
through this life and after;
and afterwards I will go to live in the Big Teepee
and sit down with the Shepherd Chief forever.[20]

As you experience your lovableness more and more profoundly, you may wish to compose your own magnificat. Like Mary (Luke 1:46-55), each of us can write a hymn of gratitude and praise to God for the blessings of love we have received and for the beautiful persons we are.

Our goal—striving to attain the fullness of love—is

to locate our ultimate identity in God and in God's love. Perhaps then we will come to the same conclusion as Thomas Merton. In answer to the question, "What is my identity?" he wrote:

> To say I am made in the image of God
> is to say that love is the reason
> for my existence, for God is love.
> Love is my true identity …
> Love is my true character.
> Love is my name.[21]

Two

A Prayer to Be Free

Leave all your worries with [God],
because [God] cares for you.
—1 Peter 5:7

The word "radical" means going to the root, getting down to essentials. People who get down to essentials and stay with them, no matter what the changes around them, are and remain radical. They are rooted in something that endures. The most radical element of our faith is the unconditional love of God. The more we internalize this truth, the greater the transformation that happens within us. Transformation has to do with freedom, freedom to live and love like Christ.

A few years ago, while making my annual eight-day retreat, I came upon a form of prayer that has literally changed my life. I call it "Freedom-Prayer." It is a prayer that can result in a greater capacity to love and the ability to receive love; it offers deliverance from those obstacles within ourselves, aspects of the false self, that keep us imprisoned.[1]

The faith involved in freedom-prayer is like the faith of a child; it expresses a child's openness and trust. It is based on the belief that God truly loves us and knows what is best for us, that God wants us to be free and wants to heal us of anything that inhibits our inner freedom. Faith is a gift, but we grow in faith each time we put our trust in God's love. In the gospels, Jesus urges people to have faith and he praises those who do (Matthew 8:10-13). He also tells us in Mark's gospel:

"Have faith in God. I assure you that whoever tells this hill to get up and throw itself in the sea and does not doubt in [his/her] heart, but believes that what [he/she] says will happen, it will be done for [him/her.] For this reason I tell you: When you pray and ask for something, believe that you have received it, and you will be given whatever you ask for" (Mark 11:22-24).

That "hill" may be fear, a resentment, or some other restriction on our freedom to live the kind of life that God wishes for us.

The best way to explain the freedom-prayer is to share how I discovered it and some of the ways I have since used it. I have applied this prayer to a variety of situations in my life: to interpersonal relationships, to my ministry, to combat fears, and even in situations where there is physical danger.

In the summer of 1982 I lived and worked among the economically poor in Tijuana, Mexico. I stayed at Casa de los Pobres, a multi-service facility for those in need of food, clothing, and medical care in Tijuana. I came to know about the Casa through our Jesuit novices who live there for short periods as part of their novitiate training. However, that summer I was the only Jesuit at the Casa. While living there, I was constantly in touch with the loving people of the city. However, I discovered in myself certain prejudices toward Mexican people. During the summer two important things happened to me: I worked through the prejudices, becoming free of their hold on me, and, as a consequence of this healing, I fell in love with the people.

This experience of love was to lead me to one of the most difficult decisions of my life. For nine years I had been living at the Jesuit School of Theology in Berkeley, in the beautiful San Francisco Bay area which I dearly loved. Berkeley was heaven for me, so many dear friends in such a lovely setting. Following the summer in Tijuana, the thought occurred to me to move my residence from northern California to San Diego in order to continue my involvement in Tijuana on a part-time basis. I struggled with this since I knew few people in the San Diego area and did not relish leaving long-time, close friends in the Bay area. However, finally, with God's grace, I asked my provincial superior for permission to move. Awaiting his answer, I returned to Casa de los Pobres during Thanksgiving for a visit. There I encountered something unexpected in myself that greatly unsettled me.

On the one hand, it was wonderful to see people I had met during the summer once again, to play with the children, to joke with teenagers, to receive hugs from men and women who had become my friends. However, I found myself gradually withdrawing emotionally from them and I did not know why. When I returned to Berkeley, a sobering question plagued me: How can I move to San Diego in this new emotional state? Three weeks later the provincial phoned to give me permission to move! The following day I began my annual retreat, and it was on this retreat that I discovered the freedom-prayer.

I was meditating on the Annunciation when I began to see the cause of my emotional withdrawal from the people of Tijuana. I recalled that at Thanksgiving there were three novices at the Casa along with myself (they had been at the Casa for over a month). During the summer I had been the only Jesuit there. The novices had become friends with many of the same people I had met during the summer, and they were receiving the same kind of affection I had experienced. Not only that, but they were getting to know my favorite children! All of a sudden I realized the cause of my withdrawal—jealousy. The "pie of affection" which had been all mine during the summer was now being split four ways! Another person might get angry when jealous; my response was to withdraw emotionally. It was a humiliating realization. It was at this point that my retreat director suggested that I pray for *freedom from the need to be special*. It is a request for humility, the kind of attitude that Mary had. I took the director's advice. Every time I felt the tendency to withdraw because of jealous feelings, I simply said the words, "I pray for freedom from the need to be special."

After the retreat was over and before I returned to Tijuana for another short visit, I discovered other incidents that triggered jealousy or urged me to be in the spotlight. It is amazing how a grace on a retreat can open one's eyes to a pattern of behavior! On each occasion, when these troublesome reactions made their appearance, I repeated the prayer I had learned on the retreat. Gradually, the tendency to feel jealous diminished. Back at Casa de los Pobres at Easter time, I had the opportunity to put this new prayer practice to the test. Once again there were novices there, different ones than before. I took the initiative this time and introduced them to my friends and eventually even to the child who was my favorite. I had been freed and could now share with others what had been abundantly given to me, and joyfully so.

As I practiced this form of prayer I began to realize that I wasn't praying never to be treated in a special way again. Over that we have no control. A key word in the prayer is "need," the *need* to be special. What is healed is the unfreedom. Thus one gradually becomes free and is at peace whether one is treated specially or not. One becomes detached from the compulsion. As a Zen Master states it, "The great way is not so difficult for those who have no preferences."

I also learned, on another occasion, a further lesson in detachment. It was a period in my life when I was especially vulnerable and needed a lot of human support. At the time I was living in a small community in which there was another man who would share with me an account of the various trials he was going through. I have been told that I am a good listener and in fact I do enjoy hearing other people's stories. In this case, I would listen in what I thought was a selfless way. However, I noticed that he never asked *me* how *I* was doing. As time went on I began to feel resentment and was tempted to take revenge: If he was not going to listen to me, then I would stop being there for him.

Now it so happened that at that time I was reading James Finley's book, *Merton's Palace of Nowhere,* in which Finley distinguishes between the true self and the false self. An aspect of my true self is my ability to enjoy listening to others. But the feeling of resentment and vengefulness was not coming from my true self. Thus, I began asking myself: *What do I need that this man is not giving me?* And I saw what it was: interest. He had no interest in me. So I applied the freedom-prayer. Every time I felt this spirit of resentment rising, or caught myself in it after the fact, I prayed for freedom from the need for him to be interested in me. Gradually the feeling of resentment diminished and I was able to be present to the man in a loving way.

Asking, "What do I need that I'm not receiving?" is an acknowledgment that part of the problem is mine. It is checking the log in one's own eye before pointing out the speck in another's (see Matthew 7:3-5). The freedom-prayer liberates us from the false self and leads to what Merton called "disinterested love." This power to love another unconditionally for his or her own sake transcends and escapes the inevitability of unhealthy self-love.[2] Again, it is not a prayer to be free from the value itself—interest, in this case—but from the *need* that springs from selfishness or self-centeredness.

Sometimes the freedom prayed for will come right away, at other times it will take awhile. Sometimes God will use the opportunity to free you from more than you asked for: for example, from another aspect of your false self that is connected with the unfreedom that led to the prayer in the first place.

I have also used the freedom-prayer in relation to fears. In 1983 I was invited to go to South Africa to give workshops on the social mission of the church. While preparing for this trip, I had ample opportunity for prayer because fear ran rampant in me. Every time I read an article on the oppressive situation in South Africa (a police state at that time) I wondered how I could possibly go there and say what I really believed about the injustices and the oppression. I began to pose a question to myself,

"What am I afraid of losing if I speak out?" I tried to name it. Then I would pray for freedom from the fear of losing whatever came to mind. I would experience the healing and move on to the next article, the next fear. My concern went from the fear of losing my film or the camera I would take with me, to the fear of physical injury if I were incarcerated for expressing my beliefs. I needed to be released from the paralyzing kinds of fear that would hinder, if not totally halt, my preaching the word of God in this potentially dangerous atmosphere. In fact, I did go to South Africa that year and not only was I free to share my insights at the various workshops, but I was also able to help people there deal with their fears.[3]

Fear is our basic emotion, and some fears can paralyze us. For example, one may feel the fear of making mistakes in public when reading or speaking. That is the time to pray for freedom from the fear of failure or rejection. Another may experience an invitation from the Lord to a radically new vocation, but backs away because of what it may cost in suffering. Pray then for freedom from fear of the cross. To quote James Finley again: "Asking how to realize the true self is much like facing a large field covered with snow that has not been walked on and asking, 'Where is the path?' The answer is to walk across it and there will be a path."[4] Many of us fear this kind of journey, for fear of doing something wrong. Pray for freedom from the fear of making a mistake, or freedom from the fear of the unknown.

Freedom is one of the main themes in the New Testament. St. Paul urges us to "remember that you have been called to live in freedom—but not a freedom that gives free rein to the flesh" (Galatians 5:13, *NAB*). I would include in "the flesh" our compulsions and our fears, our worries and anxieties, our inability to love or receive love.

The Steps Involved in Freedom-Prayer

1. I become aware of an unfreedom or of an excessive need, a way in which I find myself acting or wanting to act, from my false self. Some examples of excessive needs:

to be respected, praised, consulted, included, in control, ordered, perfect, thanked, always available, always at peace with everyone.

2. I realize I cannot become free of this aspect of my persona through my own efforts; I acknowledge that only God can free me.

3. I believe that God wants to heal me, wants me to be more like Jesus, more like Mary, more my true self—because God loves me.

4. I ask God for insight to know what it is that I need but am not receiving (or where I lack freedom). I try to *name* it. This is important for it heightens our self-knowledge and adds to our humility.

5. I ask God for freedom from the need that I have named, for example, the need to be special. I pray this phrase every time I find myself acting from the compulsion to experience that need or realize later that I have done so.

6. I leave the healing in God's hands, like a child, with complete trust that the freedom will be given to me. I go about life, leaving God to take care of the healing. Therefore, it is not necessary to repeat the prayer often during the day. I say it only at the time I discover I am acting from the unfreedom.

It is important not to doubt. If I am of two minds about what I am praying for, I can expect nothing (see James 1:6-8 and Mark 11:23). Beatrice Bruteau states this clearly in her insightful article, "The Prayer of Faith":

> Believing in the present will produce effects in the future, provided one does not doubt. Doubting is vacillation in the expectation. Genuine consent means firmness in the expectation of future experience.[5]

Freedom Creates Inner Space

As I practiced the freedom-prayer more and more, and in various aspects of my life, a curious phenomenon began to occur. A hole would appear in my consciousness, an empty space. I am, by nature, self-reflective and thus aware of changes within. I began to notice, after receiving an inner freedom, this empty space. My first reaction was panic. What was happening? Was I losing my mind? I developed a metaphor to help myself understand this. I saw my psyche as a living room. Each piece of furniture in the room represented an aspect of my false self. When God freed me from something—an excessive need, an anxiety, a fear, a self-doubt, etc.—a piece of furniture disappeared. If the unfreedom was major, the piano or the sofa went; if minor, a picture on the wall or an object on the display cabinet disappeared.

I learned to adjust to these inner changes, to the "missing furniture," by applying an image of floating from Thomas Green's book, *When the Well Runs Dry*. When we are in the water and we want to rest, we can lie back and float. To do so we have to let go. The secret of floating, Green writes, is in learning *not* to do all the things we instinctively want to do.[6] In my case, whenever panic emerged at the removal of an unfreedom and the consequent hole in my consciousness, I instinctively wanted to scramble to set things right. Instead, I learned to let go and float patiently through the necessary period of readjustment. Green tells us that floating, in the spiritual sense, means we are at home in the sea that is God, with no visible means of support except water, whose ebb and flow, whose sudden shifts, we cannot predict or control.[7] It is a matter of surrendering to the loving care of our God.

Initially, this healing process is scary because the furniture has been a part of us for many years, since we were children in some cases. And even though these are negative aspects of our personality, we are so used to having them there we may be afraid to let them go.[8]

Eventually, it seemed that all the furniture in my living room was taken away; I felt at peace in the new consciousness. As we will see in the next chapter, there was more house-cleaning to come.

Creative Freedom

It was at this time of inner transformation that a friend of mine, a Benedictine sister, introduced me to the writings of Beatrice Bruteau. Dr. Bruteau is skilled in helping people integrate the classical spiritual traditions of the East and West.[9] I found her insights a great help to understanding what was happening in me. In terms of freedom, her concept of creative freedom has special significance. She explains this notion, as she considers whether or not one is free.

> This debate often takes the form of asking us to decide between being free to choose or else being necessitated or compelled to act as we do. Here the assumption is that the only kind of freedom there is is freedom of choice, that freedom consists precisely in the act of choosing. But if we can show another meaning for "freedom," one which is still deeper and even more "free" than is choice-freedom, then the debate will have to be reassessed. In this case I have proposed the concept of "creative freedom," in which the origin and stimulation of the action is entirely in the agent, as against "choice-freedom," in which the stimulus of the act is in the agent's environment, which presents the alternatives and evokes the motive for choosing between them.[10]

While Dr. Bruteau's concentration is on freedom and the question of identity (our true identity, as we saw in chapter one), I find her insight equally appropriate to what happens as a result of the freedom-prayer. The more one is liberated, for example, from debilitating fears—of rejection, of failure, of making a mistake, of change, of intimacy, of the unknown—the more spontaneous one becomes in doing what God wants in the moment, regardless of the cost. One is free and can be led by the Holy Spirit.

An example from Jesus' life helped me to understand creative freedom. In John 8:1-11, Jesus is in the temple area in Jerusalem teaching. Some scribes and Pharisees brought a woman forward who had been caught in adultery, and made her stand in front of everyone. We pick it up from there, in John:

> "Teacher," they said to Jesus, "this woman was caught in the very act of committing adultery. In our Law Moses commanded that such a woman must be stoned to death. Now, what do you say?" They said this to trap Jesus, so that they could accuse him. But he bent over and wrote on the ground with his finger. As they stood there asking him questions, he straightened up and said to them, "Whichever one of you has committed no sin may throw the first stone at her." Then he bent over again and wrote on the ground. When they heard this, they all left, one by one, the older ones first. Jesus was left alone, with the woman still standing there. He straightened up and said to her, "Where are they? Is there no one left to condemn you?"
>
> "No one, sir," she answered.
>
> "Well then," Jesus said, "I do not condemn you either. Go, but do not sin again."

Jesus is free from the expectations of the scribes and Pharisees. He does not respond to the question they ask. Choice-freedom would mean replying directly to the woman's accusers, and the more unfree one is the more one would sugar-coat the reply so as to look good in their eyes. Jesus' response comes from his center: "the origin and stimulation of the action is entirely in the agent." He confounds the scribes and Pharisees by holding a mirror, so to speak, to their souls. They are now the ones on trial, instead of the woman. Jesus acts from this deeper freedom a second time when he does not condemn the woman, but rather treats her with compassion.

Dr. Bruteau explains this dynamic further: "Creative freedom creates what it loves instead of merely responding to it."[11] Such a person becomes "a present-into-future living being."[12] She writes, "As living, this self is in the act of creating the future from moment to moment."[13] This deeper form of freedom leads to closer union with God:

One's being is united with God's being, which is the eternal and continuous act of creative freedom, willing abundant being to all. And thus one's will is united with God's will, as being the same kind of will and the same act of will, a creative freedom that enters into all beings and dwells with them, projecting spiritual energies toward and into them that they also may be creative beings.[14]

This is what Thomas Merton means by the true self, the one who is grounded in the love of God and thus free to do what God wants.

I had a personal experience of creative freedom during a sabbatical in 1986. Since my ministry mainly involves giving retreats, I am scheduled at least a year ahead. However, I did not have a fixed plan for the sabbatical, no specific program to attend; I simply wanted to study more about prayer and issues of compassion and social justice. But, as I began this period of reflection, I found I was in a bit of a panic without the ever-present daily schedule! I prayed for the freedom to let each day, even each half-day, evolve. Gradually, I was able to let go of the need to plan ahead, and I became "a present-into-future person," "creating the future from moment to moment." It was a wonderfully peaceful experience.

A prayer that sums up the invitation to be free is called "Touch Me with Truth That Burns Like Fire" (author unknown):

Lord, send the gift of your Spirit
to fill this place
and myself
and the world.

Touch me with truth
that burns like fire,

41

with beauty that moves me like the wind;
and set me free, Lord,
free to try new ways of living,
free to forgive myself and others,
free to love and laugh and sing,
free to lay aside my burden of security,
free to join the battle for justice and peace,
free to see and listen and wonder again
at the gracious mystery of things and persons;

free to be,
to give,
to receive,
to rejoice as a child of your Spirit.

And, Lord,
teach me how to dance,
to turn around and come down where I want to be,
in the arms and heart of your people
and in you,
that I may praise and enjoy you forever.

Three

The Call to Contemplation

I … ask the God of our Lord Jesus Christ … to give
you the Spirit, who will make you wise and reveal
God to you, so that you will know [God]. I ask that
your minds may be opened to see [God's] light, so
that you will know what is the hope to which [God]
has called you … and how very great is [God's]
power at work in us who believe. This power
working in us is the same as the mighty strength
which [God] used [to raise] Christ from death.

—Ephesians 1:17-20

We read in chapter one that God's love is *the* foundation
of our life and of our identity. To come to this belief is a
primary conversion experience. The more we realize the
truth of God's love in our lives the freer we become. We
grow in awareness of the love of God in many ways but
especially through prayer.

When we first begin to pray, most of us use what is
known as discursive prayer: I tell God my problems and
the difficulties of my loved ones, or I look at the world
situation and ask God for peace and social justice, or I say
formal prayers like the Our Father, the Hail Mary, or some
favorite phrase. I may make an occasional novena, say the
Rosary, or do some special devotion. Each of these is good
prayer, for each speaks of a basic faith and trust in God.
The only problem is that in discursive prayer, I am doing
all the talking! From God's perspective it is like having a
relationship with someone who never listens. The fullness
of prayer involves both speaking *and* listening. When the

prophet Samuel was a young boy and he heard God's voice in the night, he replied, "Speak; your servant is listening" (1 Samuel 3:10). Sometimes, perhaps, we find ourselves saying, "Listen, Lord, your servant is speaking!" St. Teresa of Avila, the great Carmelite, taught that prayer is nothing else but an intimate friendship, a frequent heart-to-heart conversation with God, whom we know loves us.

As our faith develops so does our prayer. In this chapter we will consider three types of prayer: meditation on the scriptures, imaginative prayer, and centering prayer. Each method can lead us closer to God who is the source of all inner freedom.

Meditation on the Scriptures

It is important to realize that God desires to communicate with us. God wants our friendship to grow. A primary means God uses to reach us is the Bible. In this form of prayer we choose a passage from scripture. Perhaps the verses you choose are from the daily Mass readings, perhaps they express a particular theme you are interested in, like love, compassion, or hope, or perhaps you just choose something at random.[1]

Begin reading the text you have chosen, slowly. Try to savor each word, each phrase, mulling it over. Let the meaning of what you are reading go beyond your mind to your heart. When something strikes you, you may feel a new way of being with Christ, or be moved to feel God's love. You may be lifted up in the spirit, be at peace, or feel moved to do something good. Perhaps you are just happy and content to be in God's presence. This is the time to *pause*. This is God speaking directly to you in the words of scripture. Wait until you are no longer moved by the experience, then continue. Do not get discouraged if nothing seems to be happening, trust that even now God is at work in you leading you closer. After a while you may feel led to some sort of spontaneous petition, praise, or thanksgiving. End this time of reflection on the scripture by slowly reciting the Our Father, Hail Mary, or some other favorite formal prayer.

This method of prayer engages the whole person: body, mind, heart, and spirit. During the prayer one both listens and speaks to God.

Imaginative Prayer

The further we progress in the spiritual life the more our prayer becomes a process of listening. In imaginative prayer we attend to God in a more contemplative way than when we reflectively read the scriptures.

In imaginative prayer one uses a passage from the gospels to get to know Jesus more intimately. One's desire is to fall in love, or more in love, with the person of Jesus, by getting to know his personality, his values, his mind and heart. Thus, one is enabled to follow Jesus more closely. The prayer of imagination consists of taking a scene from one of the gospels and imagining yourself in the midst of what is happening. You may begin as a spectator, one of the crowd, for example, then as one of the main actors. You want to be there when the leper approaches Jesus for healing (Mark 1:40-42), when the paralytic is lowered through the roof of the house (Luke 5:17-26), with Mary and the disciples at the wedding in Cana (John 2:1-10), at the well where Jesus encounters the Samaritan woman and offers her living water (John 4:5-42). Their plight might resonate with some need for healing of your own: perhaps you are paralyzed by some fear, for example, and so you become the one who is lowered through the crowd to be touched by the healing power of the Lord.

This prayer was taught by St. Ignatius of Loyola and is known, also, as the "application of the senses," for you want to engage, as much as possible, your five senses—to look, listen, smell, taste, and touch—as you contemplate the scene. In this form of prayer, your imagination is used as an avenue to some kind of personal encounter with Jesus. Philip Sheldrake explains it this way:

Imagination is not an end in itself. Its value is that it can dispose me for an encounter with the living Christ who speaks directly to my present condition. Once that meeting between Christ and my inner desires or fears or ambiguities has begun, the process of imagining ceases to be important and should not be sustained artificially. In practice a person will be drawn into dialogue, or into silent "being with" God whose presence is now consciously felt. The imaginative phase, strictly so-called, may last for most of the period of prayer or be a relatively brief experience as a preface to extended silence.[2]

A passage that I often use on retreats is Jesus' washing the feet of the disciples (John 13:1-11). As you engage in this exercise, pause after each sentence and imagine what is being described.

Imagine the room where the Last Supper took place—how big it is, how well lighted the room is.

Notice the table, where it is situated in the room, how large it is. See how the food and the goblets of wine are placed.

You are there as a spectator.

See the disciples and Jesus reclining at the table; listen to the sound of their voices as they speak with one another. Perhaps you catch the words of a conversation.

One of the disciples notices you in the room and invites you to join them, pointing to an empty chair and a place at the table.

You say yes to this expression of hospitality and situate yourself at the table.

Smell the aroma of freshly baked bread, touch the goblet filled with wine and taste the coolness of the wine.

Suddenly, the room becomes quiet. All eyes are on Jesus, for he is standing up. Watch as he removes his outer garment, picks up a towel and ties it around himself. He pours water from a pitcher into a basin and kneels in front of the disciple reclining next to him.

There is a stunned silence in the room. You and the disciples are astonished at what you see happening before you.

Jesus is washing the feet of the disciple!

Notice the look in Jesus' eyes as he glances at the disciple, and prepares to move to the next one.

How do you feel as you see him once again kneel, wash the next disciple's feet, and dry them with the towel he has around his waist?

Jesus now comes to Peter and you listen as you hear the conversation between Jesus and Peter:

"Lord, are you going to wash my feet?"

"You may not realize now what I am doing, Peter, but later you will understand."

"You shall never wash my feet!"

"If I do not wash you, Peter, you will have no share in my heritage."

"Lord, then not only my feet, but my hands and head as well."

You watch as Jesus proceeds to wash Peter's feet.

There is only one person separating you from Peter. How do you feel as you realize that Jesus intends to wash your feet as well?

Now, Jesus is before you. Notice the expression on his face as he looks at you. Look into his eyes. If you find yourself resistant in any way to having your feet washed, ask him to free you from this obstacle to receiving his love.

Feel his hands as he massages your feet, cleanses them in the water, and then dries your feet with the towel.

What do you wish to say to him as a way of thanking him for this great act of love?

Spend some time thanking him in your heart.

Rest in his presence for as long as you wish.

This is a powerful form of prayer, one that leads both to a deeper love of Jesus and to greater self-appreciation. Here is how to proceed in the prayer of the imagination.

The Steps Involved in the Prayer of the Imagination

1. *Find a place where you are alone and uninhibited in your response to God's presence.* If you live in a family setting, you will have to exercise some creativity here. For example, a father tells how, when his six children were small, he used to pray in the bathtub! His wife would mind the children while he prayed. Fortunately they had more than one bathroom. A woman, also with little children, relates how she goes to the garage and sits in the car to pray; her husband takes care of the children until she is finished. Another woman prays in a large closet in her house, because that is where she finds the quiet.

2. *Choose a gospel story from Jesus' life.* Read the passage through once in order to familiarize yourself with the scene and the people. Imagine the place and the persons in the story. Use your five senses as appropriate to the passage. If, during the course of the time set aside for this prayer, your mind becomes distracted, bring yourself back to the scene by re-reading the story, or as much of it as you need to re-enter the prayer.

3. *Focus on the person of Jesus.* How does he look? What is he saying? How is he acting?

4. *Reflect on yourself.* Is the passage saying something to you about your own need for healing? Is it challenging you

to grow in compassion or mercy? Is it saying something to you about the cross you have to bear?

5. *Rest in the presence of God for as long as you can.*

6. *Thank God, in some way, for this time of prayer.*

It is best to be in a relaxed and peaceful posture when you pray, with harmony of body and spirit. This is not the time to practice self-denial by sitting, for example, in such a way as to cause yourself some discomfort. This will only lead to distractions and take you away from the purpose of this time with God.

The Call to Contemplation: Centering Prayer

The root of prayer is interior silence. "Be still and know that I am God," writes the psalmist (see 46:10). For many of us, silence is a foreign language. We get in the car and immediately turn on the radio. We arrive home from work and on goes the television. We go to church and promptly start reading prayers. We may have to learn how to be comfortable in the quiet. There is also an unwritten law that deeply affects our lives and inhibits our being quiet. Walter Burghardt mentions this, in his excellent article on contemplation, when he quotes the author, Walter Kerr: "Only useful activity is valuable, meaningful, moral. Activity that is not clearly useful to oneself or to others is worthless, meaningless, immoral."[3] We often feel guilty or ill at ease if we have nothing to do! But to move into contemplation not only do we have to learn the language of silence but we also have to become comfortable with *being*. It may be that we are afraid of silence because we are uncomfortable within ourselves. We may need to ask God for further healing of our self-image and to be more deeply grounded in God's unconditional love. Perhaps the fear of not being in control of our mind inhibits us, as random thoughts, some from our subconscious, come floating by. The freedom-prayer can be used here as we pray for freedom from the need to be in control.

In *The Ascent of Mount Carmel* St. John of the Cross

gives three signs that God is inviting us into a quieter form of prayer.[4] First is the discovery that we simply cannot pray in a meditative way anymore. No matter how hard we try there is no longer a sense of satisfaction in praying this way. Second, we feel a kind of resistance, or disinclination, in thinking about a passage from scripture or using our imagination even though we may have prayed these methods successfully for many years. The third and surest sign is that we long to remain quietly in the presence of God with our mind at peace.

Presently, we will consider centering prayer, a form of contemplation that helps cultivate interior silence. First, however, allow me to return to my own story.

In chapter two, I related that I lived in Tijuana, Mexico, for a summer and that while there I fell in love with the people. This experience led me to a "second conversion" (the first conversion occurred when I joined the Jesuit Order). In considering the possibility of moving my residence from the San Francisco area, in order to be closer to Tijuana, the key to being free to move came from a passage in the gospels. It is the story of the rich young man who asked Jesus what he needed to do to share in everlasting life. Jesus responded:

> "You know the commandments: 'Do not commit murder; do not commit adultery; do not steal; do not accuse anyone falsely; do not cheat; respect your father and your mother.'"
>
> "Teacher," the man said, "ever since I was young, I have obeyed all these commandments."
>
> Jesus looked straight at him with love and said, "You need only one thing. Go and sell all you have and give the money to the poor, and you will have riches in heaven; then come and follow me" (Mark 10:17-21).

Jesus' words, "Go and sell all you have and give to the poor," stared back at me from the page. The question came, "What do I have?" And the response: the Jesuit community in Berkeley which had been a wonderful source of support for many years; other friends in the San Francisco Bay area; the beauty of the natural surroundings, San Francisco itself, the Golden Gate Bridge, the Berkeley hills and parks. These were possessions of substance, part of my heart, very difficult to let go of, or even to think of leaving. "What do I have to give to the poor of Tijuana?" was the second question. The answer was simple: my time and my love. An inner freedom came to me as I reflected on this passage and the questions it evoked, one that was to have far reaching implications in the whole of my life. I "sold" what I had and moved to San Diego.

When we let go of that which is most precious to us in order to follow Christ, strange and exciting things start happening. We will likely experience some form of darkness or desert in our prayer as we adjust to the severe shift in our circumstances. If it's an accident we are coping with the desert may be our period of convalescence; if we are suddenly unemployed, enforced idleness; if we have moved to a distant location, insecurity; if we are incarcerated, fear of being physically harmed. Some of what one experiences can be explained in psychological terms: fear, insecurity, adjustment, or transition. However, it is not unusual for one's sense of God and one's way of praying to undergo a change at this time. It was shortly after I became free to ask my provincial for permission to move to southern California that the freedom-prayer was given to me. In the first four months of life in San Diego, words like abandonment, complete dependence, disorientation, and surrender characterized my time of prayer. Before the move I felt safe and secure in how I related to God. The move was a disruption in more ways than I had imagined. Yet, that is not the whole story, for God gifted me with unimagined graces.

As I gradually adjusted to living in my new home, new freedoms were given to me, especially in the affective area of my life. I was now working part-time in Tijuana among the very poor (economically speaking). I found the spontaneous and genuine love of the Mexican people a grace, for it opened my heart to love and be loved more freely. In addition to the changes in my apostolic involvement, I began to ask God for "progress in prayer." I had read this phrase in a book and the sense of it appealed to me. One of my early spiritual directors had encouraged asking God for growth in prayer. "If God wants to grant your request," he said, "he will, there is no harm in asking." Teresa of Avila counseled against hesitancy in the spiritual journey. She wrote:

> When we proceed with all this caution, we find stumbling blocks everywhere; for we are afraid of everything, and so dare not go farther. For the love of the Lord, let us make real effort: let us leave our reason and our fears in God's hands and let us forget the weakness of our nature which is apt to cause us so much worry. Our task is only to journey with good speed so that we may see the Lord.[5]

As a result of asking God for progress in prayer, I was led to pray what is known as centering prayer.

The prayer we call centering is described in *The Cloud of Unknowing* by an anonymous mystic of the fourteenth century. The author wrote:

> This is what you are to do: lift your heart up to the Lord, with a gentle stirring of love desiring him for his own sake and not for his gifts. Center all your attention and desire on him and let this be the sole concern of your mind and heart. Do all in your power to forget everything else, keeping your thoughts and desires free from involvement with any of God's creatures or their affairs whether in general or in particular.[6]

Centering prayer is imageless awareness, beyond words, beyond imagination, beyond discursive thought. Even a spiritual insight is considered a distraction in this kind of prayer. This method of communion with God consists of letting go of everything that comes to one's consciousness: an emotion, an image, a memory, a thought, even the awareness of being at peace. We do this in order to enter into a pure act of adoration of God. It is not a matter of repressing our thoughts, but of being detached from them. Thomas Keating explains: "We do not deny or repress what is in our consciousness. We simply accept the fact of whatever is there and go beyond it, not by effort, but by letting go of whatever is there."[7] He suggests the image of a river:

> It is a question of allowing our ordinary thoughts to recede into the background and to float along the river of consciousness without our noticing them, while we direct our attention toward the river on which they are floating. We are like someone sitting on the bank of a river and watching the boats go by. If we stay on the bank, with our attention on the river rather than on the boats, the capacity to disregard thoughts as they go by will develop, and a deeper kind of attention will emerge.[8]

There are two theological thoughts that underlie centering prayer and other forms of contemplation: God is beyond anything I can conceive in my mind; God can be grasped by love, but never by concepts.

Centering prayer is a prayer of *the present moment.* I center my attention in the now moment by means of a sacred word or phrase, one that expresses my intention of opening and surrendering to God.[9] This word, or phrase, is called a mantra (from the Sanskrit: *man*—to think, *tra*—to liberate): liberation of the mind from sense images and concepts. I might use the name "Jesus" for my sacred word, or "Spirit," or "Love," and so forth. I might wish to use a short phrase, such as, "God is Love," "God loves me," "Jesus, have mercy," or some other phrase that expresses my intention to open myself to God. It can be a help to repeat this word or phrase in rhythm with your breathing, though this is not necessary. I focus on the word and return to it when the inevitable distractions come. As to the amount of time to set aside for this form of prayer, Thomas Keating suggests: "Twenty to thirty minutes is the minimum amount of time necessary for most people to establish interior silence and to get beyond their superficial thoughts. You may be inclined to remain longer. Experience will teach you what the right time is."[10] Writers on contemplative prayer suggest praying in this way either before a meal or an hour and a half afterward. This is so because the metabolism of the body is affected by the quieter forms of prayer; it is best to do so on an empty stomach.

Steps Involved in Centering Prayer

1. Simply sit, relaxed and quiet, enjoying your own inner *calm* and *silence*. For a few minutes, *listen* to God's presence and allow yourself to be touched by it.

2. After a time, perhaps a single word or short phrase will come, one that captures your response to God's inner presence. Let this word or phrase represent the fullness of God to you. Repeat it in rhythm with your breathing if this is possible for you.

3. Center all your attention and desire on God, leaving your faculties at peace, allowing God to draw you into a perfect prayer of adoration, love, and praise. Let it happen. Whenever you become aware of any feelings, thoughts, or images simply return to your word or short phrase.

4. In coming out of prayer, move slowly to silent awareness and then a conscious interior prayer, such as the Our Father, speaking the words slowly, savoring the words and meaning, entering into them.

Mahatma Gandhi was a zealous advocate of this form of prayer. He claimed it brought with it the most extraordinary benefits for spirit, mind, and body. He claimed to have overcome all his fears simply through ceaseless repetition of God's name, which he recited with all his heart, soul, and mind during the time of prayer.

God led me into the practice of centering prayer and

for a while I found it easy to repeat the name, Jesus, with few distractions. However, as time went on the "little boats on the river of consciousness" (distracting thoughts) began to plague me. With some reflection, I noticed a pattern to some of these distractions. I was trying to be in the present moment, but my mind would be planning the day ahead, and there was a kind of "natural consolation" in the imagined order to all the activities coming up. I decided to utilize the freedom-prayer again. I prayed for freedom from the need to plan ahead and I said this prayer every time I noticed that I was in the future, in my mind, rather than in the present. Gradually, this form of distraction diminished and the prayer became quieter.[11] I believe one can use the freedom-prayer in relation to whatever pattern of distractions one discovers. Later, freedom from the need to plan ahead was to have an effect on my whole day as the time outside of formal prayer became more contemplative as well. As I mentioned in chapter two, this is not a prayer to be free from the thing itself, for example, planning ahead. Obviously, we need to do that. It is a prayer for release from the compulsion, from that which takes us out of the present moment when we are trying to center all our attention on God.

Sometimes our distractions in prayer are startling. Thomas Merton gave good advice concerning the odd images that occasionally emerge:

> After a while, the doors of the subconscious mind fall ajar and all sorts of curious figures begin to come waltzing about on the scene. If you are wise you will not pay any attention to these things: remain in simple attention to God and keep your will peacefully directed to him in simple desire, while the intermittent shadows of this annoying movie go about in the remote background. If you are aware of them at all it is only to realize that you refuse them.[12]

What one needs at such a time is a good sense of humor. One retreatant, a computer analyst, shared with me that when he tried to sit quietly in the presence of God, pink elephants and purple dinosaurs came dancing into his head! He was completely unnerved by this, and was tempted to give up centering prayer. However, with his sense of humor and patience, he was able to weather this trial, and proceed in the prayer. He found it helpful to talk about his distractions and to find out he is not alone in experiencing such images. The images gradually diminish as one becomes more accustomed to the inner quiet and may eventually completely disappear.

After practicing centering prayer for about six months, I encountered another obstacle. For years prior I had meditated on the scriptures, engaging my mind, coming to insights, and having a feeling of accomplishment. In this quieter form of prayer, my mind was not being used, that is, the rational part of the mind. Instead of doing, I was being. The emphasis was on listening, in the quiet. My intuitive faculties were opening up. However, I felt like I was wasting time—nothing seemed to be happening. The thought came to return to my old way of praying, back to meditating on the Bible. It was at that moment that the following insight came to me: As an active person, you know how effective your prayer is by the *quality* of your life. Look at what is happening outside the formal time of prayer.

At the time, my ministry was going quite well. People were experiencing conversion on the retreats I gave and I had an overall sense of well-being and wholeness. This is a key insight for centering prayer, because during the time for prayer the mind is quiet. There is no feeling of accomplishment (except, perhaps, that one actually stays with it for thirty minutes, despite the various distractions one may encounter). The proper question, then, for this quieter form of prayer is: Am I growing in love, compassion, patience, assertiveness (or perhaps humility), care for the wounded in society, and so forth? You know by the quality of your life that what you are doing for those twenty or thirty minutes a day is prayer. The quality of your life may also be judged by whether or not you have come through a crisis with your faith still intact, your trust in a loving God more secure, and your hope more grounded.

The sacred word, in centering prayer, points to a deeper level of interior silence. There is a level of attention that is beyond the sacred word. "Only when you pass beyond the word into pure awareness is the process of interiorization complete."[13] Here is even closer union with God. "The experience of interior peace is the sacred word at its deepest level. You are experiencing the end of the journey toward which the sacred word is pointing."[14] For most of us, however, this state does not last for the rest of our lives. Even the way we pray may periodically change. The important thing is to be open to how the Spirit wants us to pray. And, in the practice of quiet prayer distractions have a way of interrupting even the most devout person, sending us back to the sacred word.

Centering prayer is both a method toward the deeper stillness, and true prayer at the same time. It is a gesture of receptivity and surrender. People in the Charismatic Renewal can come to this interior silence through speaking in tongues. The quiet is beyond speaking in tongues just as it is beyond the sacred word. In centering prayer, Thomas Keating points out:

> You may reach a point where you no longer think of the sacred word at all. So long as you experience the undifferentiated, general, and loving presence of God beyond any thought, don't go back to the sacred word. You are already at your destination.[15]

Quiet prayer is receptive, not active. The emphasis is on being rather than doing. As we will see, in chapter four, such prayer involves the intuitive faculties of the mind rather than the analytical, rational, ones. Quiet prayer is an experience of pure faith and, ultimately, pure being: the I AM of God meeting the I AM of me.

Some Practical Considerations

Regardless of the method of prayer we choose—meditation on the scriptures, imaginative prayer, or centering prayer—our body is an important part of this time spent with God. If we are tense, nervous, or under stress it will affect how we pray. Simple exercises such as a brief walk outside, a swim, or a slow walk in one's room (taking short steps, walk in a circle until you feel relaxed), can help us unwind and prepare us for prayer. A retreatant told me how she does needlepoint in order to calm down. Some find it helpful to do yoga exercises to calm their emotions and ready the body. The Zen teacher, Thich Nhat Hanh gives some excellent ideas on slowing the body in his book, *A Guide to Walking Meditation*.[16] Jogging around the block can also undo the kinks in our system.

Music is an aid to quieting the spirit. A mother of three young children shared how she uses wordless music to bring herself to a peaceful place within after a hectic day with her family. It is best to listen to music where you do not know the theme, so as not to be distracted by a familiar melody. Artists such as Mike Rowland, Kitaro, Steve Bergman, and William Ackerman have composed meditational music to help one relax.[17] Some people relate that they successfully use this kind of music throughout their time of prayer when their mind is a jumble of thoughts.

It is important to realize that prayer is not a running away from the world but a deeper embracing of it. Thomas Merton wrote: "We do not go into the desert to escape people but to learn how to find them; we do not leave them in order to have nothing more to do with them, but to find out the way to do them the most good."[18] When we practice centering prayer and enter into the deeper quiet that it can lead us to, we go beyond thoughts and images. This is not the time to think about problems in the world. How, then, does one stay connected to suffering people? William Johnston, S.J. suggests keeping up on the "scriptures of the world," the daily news that comes to us via the radio, television, newspapers, and magazines. From my own experience, I would add, have some regular personal contact with wounded people, be they in poverty or sickness. This involvement affects our prayer, for whatever we read or witness enters into our subconscious and thus into our prayer, on an implicit as well as explicit level. It is also helpful to offer the time of prayer for some persons in need or some place in turmoil. One can think of many such intentions: the homeless, refugees, the unemployed, those who are physically or emotionally handicapped, people with AIDS or some other terminal disease, civil wars, healing of the planet, and so on.

Finally, the following practical suggestions are meant to assist you as your prayer-style becomes more contemplative or quiet.

Suggestions for Quiet Prayer

1. Pray the way that feels best for you; do not be afraid to experiment with new ways of praying.

2. Read the Bible, especially the gospels, outside quiet prayer, in order to stay connected with the person of Jesus.

3. Read one book on prayer a year; this will help your prayer life. If you are an active person, in the midst of the world, read books by monastic authors—like Thomas Merton, Teresa of Avila, Thomas Keating, John of the Cross—but take what is appropriate to your spirituality and leave the rest. The same for books from the East; not everything in them is for those in the West, and vice versa.

4. Do not completely give up former ways of praying. Some days it is not possible to do centering or quiet prayer. The Spirit may lead you into meditation on the scriptures, or prayer using your imagination, and you want to be free to follow the Spirit's lead.

Four

Putting on the Mind and Heart of Christ

> But all those things that I might count as profit I
> now reckon as loss for Christ's sake. Not only those
> things; I reckon everything as complete loss for the
> sake of what is so much more valuable, the
> knowledge of Christ Jesus my Lord. For his sake I
> have thrown everything away; I consider it all as
> mere garbage, so that I may gain Christ and be
> completely united with him.
>
> *—Philippians 3:7-9*

Many authors on prayer today write about the changes in
consciousness that happen as a result of closer union with
God. Abbot Thomas Keating, for example, writes of "a
restructuring of consciousness" that is one effect of contemplation.[1] Basil Pennington in his book, *Centered Living*, devotes
a chapter to the transformation of consciousness and a
chapter to pure consciousness.[2] In discussing the question
of personal identity, Beatrice Bruteau shows how the less
one identifies with one's descriptions, the more free does
one's "praying consciousness" become.[3] In chapter one
we considered the temptation we have to put our self-
worth in what describes us: the amount of salary we
receive, the section of the city or county we live in, the
successes we enjoy, and so forth. These are true insofar as
we keep them on the level of description; they become
"idols" when we place our identity in them. Our spiritual
journey consists of many conversion experiences that
bring us closer to imitating Christ by putting our ultimate
identity in the love God has for us.

While it is true that one comes into a different level of awareness, or consciousness, through the practice of contemplation, I found that frequent use of the freedom-prayer also results in profound interior changes. Recall the image described in chapter two: how gradually all the "furniture" in my "living room," that is, the various aspects of my false self (all the manifestations of the illusory self that I was aware of at the time) had to be removed by God's grace. Eventually, I felt at peace in this new consciousness. The inner freedom I experienced had a profound effect on the whole of my life.

Sometimes, as one progresses in the spiritual journey, God enters the soul in an unexpected and powerful way, grounding the soul in love so intensely that the way the person sees life changes dramatically. Deep gratitude is the appropriate response for such a gift. The tendency for most of us, however, is to cling to the experience, hoping that God will repeat it. The words of William Blake are instructive here:

> He who binds to himself a joy
> does the winged life destroy.
> But he who kisses the joy as it flies
> lives in eternity's sunrise.[4]

In other words, if we cling to a particular experience of God's love, we may miss the new surprise of love that God wants to give us.

Unloading the Unconscious

For the Christian, it is important to remember that all the graces we receive stem from the resurrection of Jesus. His victory over death and over the forces of evil confirms our belief that *his kingdom will never be destroyed,* neither in general nor in our heart. This realization of the power flowing from his resurrection (Philippians 3:10) and an ever deepening acceptance of God's unconditional love are what give us the courage we need to enter into new states of consciousness. Sometimes these changes in our interior life are filled with joy and peace. However, at other times we are faced with a disturbing darkness or desert.

Consider, for example, what Thomas Keating calls "the unloading of the unconscious," a dynamic that occurs through the regular practice of quiet prayer.[5] The deep peace that comes with contemplative prayer releases emotional blocks within us, some of which go back to earliest childhood. Insights into the negative side of our psyche emerge. The root causes of our unfreedoms rise to our consciousness. This happens because we have let go of control, and we are giving God permission to heal us at a deeper level. We may have already experienced inner healing of some emotional wound from the past, and here we are face-to-face with it again! The temptation is to be discouraged at this recurrence. It is important to realize that the process of inner healing is like going to the dentist because of an aching tooth. The dentist examines the tooth and discovers a cavity that needs to be cleaned and filled. Years later we return to the dentist because pain has recurred in the same tooth. "Aha," the dentist says, "what you need now is a root canal!" The root canal is symbolic of the deeper healing in our unconscious that needs to happen if we are to truly put on the mind and heart of Christ.

It is my experience that this "unloading of the unconscious" happens outside the formal time of prayer, too. God leads us into situations where, if we cooperate, wounds from our past are healed. Memories of hurtful actions done to us by another (or others) are released, triggered by some event in the present. Such was the case in my life when I met someone who had a dark side to his personality similar to my father's. Every time I was with this person, something in his behavior would remind me of a destructive way my father had behaved when I was young. As each memory came back to me, I brought it to God for healing.[6] The daily Mass readings, at that time, spoke directly to what I was going through. Passages such as Isaiah 35:4-7 (*NAB*):

Say to those whose hearts are frightened:
Be strong, fear not!
Here is your God ...
[Who] comes to save you.

and, Psalm 146:7: "The LORD sets prisoners free," gave me courage and reassured me of God's loving presence in this time of purification and transformation. (We will return to this theme later when we consider the Dark Night of the Soul.) I had been praying in a contemplative way for over five years when this healing of hurtful memories occurred. When one is going through a time of purification, it is important to have another person to talk with, a spiritual companion whose advice we value, who can help us not to be overwhelmed by the memories that surface.

Geoffrey Williams writes of this time of inner healing in terms of the pain involved, "The contemplative does not love pain, but realizes that the pain is healing because it is felt only when the hurt covered with the scab of fear is touched by the love of the Father."[7] Again, I find the freedom-prayer helpful here. When my fear of the possible pain involved threatens to immobilize me, I ask God for freedom from the fear of the cross.

The Present Moment

Contemplation is a way of life. The inner stillness born in the quiet time of prayer spills over and permeates one's interpersonal relationships, one's work, and one's play. One lives more and more in the present moment, what Ken Wilber calls, "the eternal present." As he explains:

What is a timeless moment? What instant is without date or duration? What moment is not just quick or short-lived in time, but absolutely without time? Odd as these questions initially seem, most of us would have to admit that we have known moments, peak moments, which seemed indeed to lie so far beyond time that the past and the future melted away into obscurity. Lost in a sunset; trans-fixed by the play of moonlight on a crystal dark pond which possesses no bottom; floated out of self and time in the enraptured embrace of a loved one; caught and held still-bound by the crack of thunder echoing through mists of rain. Who has not touched the timeless? What do all of these experiences have in common? Time appears suspended in all of these experiences because we are totally absorbed in the *present moment.*[8]

In the spiritual life we call this experience of time-lessness the "sacrament of the present moment." It is a change of consciousness for in the *now* moment there is neither past nor future. There is only God and the person. And, there is what some writers call "unity conscious-ness": an experience of connectedness to all that exists.[9]

To illustrate the shift of consciousness to *the present moment,* allow me to return to my own journey.

I mentioned in chapter three, how, shortly after moving to San Diego, which was a traumatic dislocation for my whole being, I began asking God for progress in prayer. The first change I noticed, after making this request, was a difference in the way I prayed: from an analytical style, meditating on a passage from the Bible, to a contemplative method, centering prayer. My mind shifted at times from busy to blank! I still used the freedom-prayer when needed.

My everyday consciousness started to be affected by the changes in the formal prayer times. At times I felt a great sense of clarity: seeing, hearing, my sense of smell, all became more acute. I felt more alive in my ministry and was encouraged by the positive comments of retreatants as they, too, were benefiting from the fruits of my prayer. I was fearful, too, of the sometimes startling shifts in my consciousness. It was in this overall state of mind, alter-nating between clarity and confusion, that I entered into my annual eight-day retreat that year, intuitively aware that God was going to use this time to teach me how to pray a new way.

The retreat took place in the mountains, in a cabin owned by some friends of mine. I was alone. It was November. The air was crisp and the trees were beginning to lose their leaves. As I began this eight-day period of seclusion I prayed for freedom from all anxiety and asked God for the ability to just *be* in the quiet. I longed for greater union with God. God strengthened me with the insight that nothing could overpower his love for me. I was encouraged by this realization and was able to let go of expectations and of a fear of the unknown, which had surfaced in the days immediately preceding the retreat.

On the third day of the retreat something unusual happened. I sat for each one-hour prayer period without a single word entering my mind. Usually, at least part of the time, I would be struggling with a myriad of distractions while trying to be still. The following day, not only did I not have any thoughts during prayer but I had no feelings either. My emotions were still. There was not even a feeling of peace, just an emptiness. On the fifth day, the absence of thoughts and feelings was joined by a third faculty, my memory. I sat through each hour of being present to God with no thoughts, no feelings, no memory. It was not until after each prayer period that I wrote down what had occurred during it. During the prayer my mind was empty, there seemed to be a darkness, or curtain, which thought could not bridge. In the afternoon of the fifth day, I prayed outside. I sat with the sun on my face, my eyes closed. Because of the absence of thoughts, feelings, and memory, the only indication to me that I actually existed was in the sounds I heard—water dripping, a bird chirping, the whine of an electric saw in the distance—and the awareness of the sun's heat on my face. There was no sense of past or future, just now.

I had brought a borrowed book with me, *The Experience of No-Self* by Bernadette Roberts, which I intended to return to its owner on the way back from the retreat. A few weeks before coming up the mountain for this time of prayer, I had tried reading the book but had trouble following the author's theme and had given up on it. On the evening of the fifth day, after having experienced the absence of thoughts, feelings, and memory, I felt inclined to pick up the book. I looked at the table of contents and saw a chapter titled, "The Silent Mind," which I recalled having noticed before though I had not read the chapter. As I read this chapter of the book, such clarity of understanding came to me about what I had been experiencing in the past three days that I keenly felt God's presence in the room. God was educating me: teacher to student.

Bernadette Roberts writes about the mechanism of self-consciousness. Her notion of no-self is, "the breaking up of a self-conscious system whereby the mind can no longer see itself as an object."[10] She writes:

> Once the mind can no longer reflect on itself, all energy or movement of the self is gone; the feelings and emotions are in silence; the memory has been so denuded that the past is lifeless with no continuum at all. From here on, each small event becomes the totality of the moment, and when this moment is over, it too has no continuum. Introspection becomes impossible; and projection is also out of the question since we can no longer endow any object with the usual values, meanings, and purposes.[11]

She continues:

> The thoughts that now come to mind do not arise from within, but originate "off the top," so to speak, and then, only when dealing with the obvious data at hand at any given time.[12]

This is a perfect description of what I had just experienced on the retreat: a mysterious kind of silence. Roberts reassured me that I had not stopped thinking altogether, but now my thoughts were more spontaneous; distracting and irrelevant thoughts were gone. In this space I was conscious of only the now moment, the immediate present. I had already begun noticing that what was happening (or not happening in my mind, emotions, and memory) during the prayer periods was spilling over into the whole day. The planning ahead that I was so used to doing was absent and I simply went about doing my chores—cooking, cleaning the cabin, raking the leaves—as necessary. Looking back, now, I see a similarity between thinking "off the top" and "creative freedom": "a present-into-future living being ... in the act of creating the future from moment to moment."[13]

In any change in consciousness there is a time of adjustment until one becomes at ease in the new state. In terms of what happened to me on the retreat mentioned above, Bernadette Roberts describes this period of realignment, "It takes a while to adjust to a new way of life wherein one discovers that the basic structure of the mind and its faculties remain intact and perfectly functional, but functional in a new way."[14] What is needed at such a time is patience, and trust in the loving God who is responsible for this new way of being.

Christ-consciousness

For as long as I can remember, I have offered my sufferings—physical, emotional, spiritual—for the needs of others. I remember my family and their struggles. I think of friends who are going through a crisis or a serious illness. Then my focus expands. I have worked in the African-American community, been to South Africa twice, and now spend a lot of time among those who are economically poor in Tijuana, Mexico. This personal contact has led me to keep these peoples in mind whenever I am undergoing an experience of purification or enduring some suffering. Like St. Paul, I find meaning in the suffering I endure for others (Colossians 1:24).

There is an awareness implicit in offering one's trials for the good of others: that we are all (including the earth and all other living creatures) intimately connected. The Christian names this reality "Christ-consciousness." In his analogy of the body with Christ, St. Paul wrote,

We have many parts in the one body, and all these parts have different functions. In the same way, though we are many, we are one body in union with Christ, and we are all joined to each other as different parts of one body (Romans 12:4-5).

Thus, when one suffers, all suffer; when one rejoices, all are happy (1 Corinthians 12:26). It is love which binds us together: the love of Christ for all, the love we have for one another, the love we have for our planet. This is a special kind of unity, a union of all things in Christ: Jesus Christ, the first-born of all creatures, in whom everything in heaven and on earth was created, the one who is before all else that is, in whom everything continues in being, he who is the first-born of the dead, he who reconciled everything in his person by means of the cross (Colossians 1:15-20). He offered his life that all might be free. To enter into his heart on the cross is to feel the pain of every sadness, every crisis, every act of injustice and violence, every sin, personal and social, that ever happened or will happen. Each Christian enters into the heart of Christ through baptism. We each feel the intensity of his compassion for the world according to the graces God gives us and the capacity we have to receive them. But we can grow in our sensitivity to the needs of others—our brothers and sisters, our earth, and all living creatures.

On the sixth day of the retreat mentioned in the previous section, after God helped me to understand the silence I had entered into, I felt a strong desire to join with Jesus in his feelings for the world: righteous anger at injustice, anguish and compassion for those in pain, gladness and joy for courageous acts of integrity. I decided to watch the evening news on television and was moved to tears a number of times when I saw scenes of people struggling for their dignity. Later, as I celebrated Mass, I felt a new sense of unity with all who suffer. The prayer of silence did not lead me to an abandonment of the world, but rather to a deeper immersion into it.

In Christ-consciousness we are united with the suffering Christ who is suffering now: in the person with AIDS, in the aborted fetus, in the pain of men and women in divorce, in the humiliation of a woman who is raped, in the shame of a drug addict, in the child dying from famine. "When one suffers, all suffer." In Christ-consciousness we feel the pain of the earth when it is despoiled; we sorrow over toxic waste and air pollution, over deforestation and the destruction of the species. But in Christ-consciousness we also rejoice in the actions of loving people as they reach out to the hurting ones with care and concern; we take hope from courageous endeavors to make the world a more just home for all of God's creatures. In the consciousness of Christ, we see the world through his eyes, hear through his ears, and feel with his heart. It is the risen Christ with whom we are united in compassion and joy. Just as he has not forgotten us in our times of trial, so too do we keep in prayer his suffering brothers and sisters.

"The Zen master 'sits' for the universe," writes William Johnston in *Silent Music*. He explains:

> This is not, I believe, just pious talk. It has a basis in psychology and even, perhaps, in physics. Because contemplation entails an expansion of mind, a loss of self, an entrance into altered states of consciousness, a thrust into a dimension beyond time and space, in such wise that not only one's spirit but his/her very psyche and body become somehow cosmic....[15]

For the Christian, the original cosmic person is Jesus Christ. It is Christ in his glory. We participate in this universal dimension as followers of Christ.

> Any Christian who sincerely prays is becoming one with the universal Christ in a process that reaches its climax in resurrection, the ultimate universalization of humanity. All knowledge and love open us up to new areas of experience by which we live in others and are necessarily affected

by their joys and sufferings. This is particularly true of mystical knowledge and love. For this goes beyond images and concepts to a deeper level of awareness wherein we are one with the person we love.[16]

The effect of Christ-consciousness is poignantly suggested in the following poem by Ken Eckel:

RINGS OF FIRE

From a source hidden
Pulses new freedom
Former untapped springs flowing

My being warmed
All parts realizing
Experiencing
Their true function
Touching others …
Creating a ring …
Spreading other new rings …
Rings of burning love.

It seems the heart
Touched unlimited new warmth
New vistas
New unquenchable
Fire![17]

Five

Intuition and Prayer

Jesus took with him Peter, James, and John, and led them up a high mountain, where they were alone. As they looked on, a change came over Jesus, and his clothes became shining white—whiter than anyone in the world could wash them. Then the three disciples saw Elijah and Moses talking with Jesus. Peter spoke up and said to Jesus, "Teacher, how good it is that we are here! We will make three tents, one for you, one for Moses, and one for Elijah." He and the others were so frightened that he did not know what to say.

—Mark 9:2-6

Intuitive Knowledge

We saw in chapter three that the root of prayer is interior silence. We also considered two theological truths that lead us into contemplative prayer: God is beyond anything I can conceive in my mind, and, God can be grasped by love, never by concepts. Contemplation, and the changes in consciousness that evolve from it, is a loving appreciation of the real without the use of the rational mind.

Recent research indicates that the brain is composed of two hemispheres: the left and the right. Thomas Blakeslee points out that each half of the brain has its own separate train of conscious thought and its own memories: the two sides of the brain think in fundamentally different ways.[1] The left-brain, or rational hemisphere, is described as aggressive, dominant, and masculine. From this half of the brain come math, science, language, abstract or analytical thought, logical deductions—concepts separated from concrete reality. This side of the brain is characterized as *doing*. The right-brain, or intuitive hemisphere, is described as passive, receptive, and feminine. From this half of the brain come art, drama, music, poetry, dance, symbolic expression—a vision of the whole. This side of the brain is characterized as *being*. In terms of practical, daily life, Thomas Blakeslee offers this example of these two halves of the brain in operation:

> If we take the plans for a house we want built to an experienced contractor, he may glance over them for about ten minutes and tell us what it will cost and how long it will take. This is an *intuitive* judgment. Another approach he could use would be to add up every item on the bill of materials, calculate the price, one item at a time, then schedule each stage of the construction and estimate building time.[2]

Both ways of thinking are real knowledge. In terms of prayer, discursive prayer is left-brain contact with God, while contemplation is right-brain communion with the Absolute. This is the *Yin* and *Yang* of Chinese philosophy: "*Yin* stands for the feminine, intuitive mind, for the silence; *Yang*, on the other hand, is the rational, masculine intellect, the logos (word)."[3]

It is important to see intuition as real knowledge. There is a tendency in Western culture, with its emphasis on analysis, to view the intuitive as inferior to the rational way of thinking. For those who are skeptical of the value of right-brain knowledge, two noted scientists have something of value to offer. Max Planck, the father of quantum theory, wrote, "The creative scientist must have a vivid intuitive imagination for new ideas not generated by deduction, but by artistically creative imagination."[4] And Albert Einstein said, "My understanding of the fundamental laws of the universe did not come out of my rational mind."[5]

The most thorough explanation of the value of intuition in our prayer life that I have read is from the book

The Marriage of East and West, by Bede Griffiths. Dom Bede writes:

> It is the purpose of every genuine religion to reveal this transcendent mystery (of God) and to teach the way to its attainment. But this revelation is given not to the rational but to the intuitive mind, and the way to discover it is not by argument but by self-surrender, the opening of the self to its eternal ground.... When we penetrate beyond the rational mind, we come upon a deeper self, a self that takes hold of our whole being, body and soul, and draws us into its infinite being.[6]

Let us take a closer look at this indispensable faculty called intuition.

Simple intuitions are hunches, a "gut feeling" for or against something, vague momentary flashes of understanding. "When we know something intuitively," writes Frances Vaughan, "it invariably has the ring of truth; yet often we do not know *how* we know what we know."[7] She explains further:

> At any given moment one is conscious of only a small portion of what one knows. Intuition allows one to draw on that vast storehouse of unconscious knowledge that includes not only everything that one has experienced or learned, either consciously or subliminally, but also the infinite reservoir of the collective or universal unconscious, in which individual separateness and ego boundaries are transcended.[8]

Intuition cannot be produced; it has to be allowed to happen. The more rational a person is, the more resistance there will be to the kind of surrender needed, because the rational mind, aggressive and dominating as it is, wants to be in control. There is also, as Thomas Keating points out, a tendency to repress the intuitive way of thinking. He writes:

> Our contemporaries in the Western world have a

special problem with discursive meditation because of the ingrained inclination to analyze things
beyond all measure.... This conceptual hang-up of
modern Western society impedes the spontaneous
movement from reflection to spontaneous prayer
and from spontaneous prayer to interior silence
(wonder and admiration).[9]

Let me illustrate this movement to spontaneous
prayer and interior silence with a personal experience.

I spent part of my 1986 sabbatical in Ireland. While
there I traveled to the West, to Connemara, for a few days
holiday. Early one Sunday morning I drove to the town of
Clifden, a lovely place that sits at the head of an ocean inlet.
I chose a bench near the water and sat down. From there I
could see little boats bobbing on the bay. Across the inlet
there were cows grazing on green hillsides. Morning
clouds partially blocked an otherwise deep blue sky. The
town was away to my left, barely visible behind some
trees. My disposition that morning was a determined one.
For a couple of days I had been asking God to break
through an inner silence my prayer had brought me to.
The resurrection had also been on my mind; I had a desire
to know it, or experience it, more fully in my life.

On the previous Tuesday, the first reading at Mass
was from Ephesians: "I pray that [God] will bestow on you
gifts in keeping with the riches of [God's] glory. May [God]
strengthen you inwardly through the working of [the]
Spirit" (3:16, *NAB*). As I sat on the wooden bench, I tried
to *think* my way into feeling the joy of the resurrection.
Nothing happened and I began to feel discouraged. Then
a curious thing occurred; something in my consciousness
urged me to let go of the thinking and just be. I found this
difficult at first. All of a sudden my eyes and ears were
affected by an intense clarity. I became clearly aware of the
glory of God in everything around me. A phrase came to
me and I repeated it after each realization. The phrase was:
"Your glory is here, Lord." I had a pad of paper with me
and wrote down each manifestation of God's glory after

being with it in my consciousness for a while. The periodic writing did not interrupt what was happening. This is what I wrote, feeling very much at peace as I did so:

Your glory is here, Lord,
in the pony and its whinny,
in the fisherman setting out in his boat,
in the patch of blue sky,
in the little boat swaying in the water,
in the town rimmed by the bay, its two church
    spires evident from where I sit,
in the sun that is struggling to appear,
in the clouds that hide its rays.

Your glory is here, Lord,
in the white birds that dive to the sea,
in the cat of gold that walks by where I sit,
in the mooing of the cows in the pasture on
    the other side of the water,
in a rooster's cry,
and in the rays of the sun coming through
    the clouds,
in my tears of joy
as I realize
your glory is right here
before my eyes, Lord.

Your glory is here, Lord,
in the sound of the water as it nudges the boats,
in the sound of the wind breezing through the
    trees,
in the color of a flower as it rises from a rock wall,
in the stony hillside that faces the town,
in the sounds of the morning—
    bees buzzing,
    birds chattering,
    water lapping,
    a dog barking,
in a town awakening on Sunday morning,
in my breathing.

By my letting go of trying to *make* prayer happen (the rational way), God was able to open the eyes of my heart to see and experience the resurrection all around me. This form of prayer experience is not inevitable when we let go of thinking, for it is a gratuitous gift from God, but at least it is possible.

Both hemispheres of the brain, the intuitive and the rational, exist in everyone. It is not unusual, however, for one dimension to be less developed or even repressed. We have seen how in the West intuition tends to be devalued. It is potentially available to us all, but it is important to know what opening up to the intuitive involves. Frances Vaughan writes:

> If one chooses to pay attention to intuition, one can certainly expand awareness of it. Learning to awaken intuition, however, is paradoxical, since intuitive experiences tend to occur spontaneously and too much effort is apt to interfere with the process. Yet although one cannot *make* intuition happen, there is much one can do to *allow* it to happen.[10]

In my own journey I became more aware of right-brain (intuitive) thinking at the age of forty when I began to learn how to interpret my dreams. The timing of this discovery would make developmental psychologists happy as they commonly teach that integration on all levels of a person's psyche begins happening in mid-life. In dream analysis, one writes down each object that was in the dream—each person, place, and thing—spending some time with each symbol, not thinking about it but writing down the first thoughts that come to mind about each. The meaning of a dream does not come through the process of logical deduction, but by listening at a deep level to one's unconscious as it speaks through the symbols.[11]

Intuition involves surrender; the mind has to let go of rational ways of thinking for intuition to happen. My power of listening, an essential aspect of the intuitive, has increased a hundred-fold through involvement with

Mexican people in Tijuana, Mexico. I am not fluent in Spanish. This forces me to pay close attention to what people are saying to me. Often, when I have trouble following the words, I am able to understand a person's message by his or her facial expression, body language, or tone of voice. This handicap with the Spanish language has been a key avenue for the development of my intuition!

Both the rational and the intuitive ways of thinking are important. Just as one can be overdeveloped in the left-brain so also in the right-brain. Bede Griffiths explains:

> Both reason and intuition by themselves are defective.... Intuition by itself is blind. It is an obscure awareness of the self in the experience of the world. The intuition easily becomes swamped by the emotions.[12]

Frances Vaughan concurs:

> Holding the rational in abeyance (while letting your intuition awaken) should not be confused with turning it off, however, as your rational, discriminating judgment is essential to checking the validity of intuitive perceptions and evaluating the process.[13]

What is needed is integration, a "marriage," to use Bede Griffiths' term, between reason and intuition. We in the West, with our over-emphasis on science and reason, need to "find the path of self-realization which has been followed for centuries in the East."[14] The Eastern path is steeped in the intuitive: in contact with the unconscious, at home in the inner silence that transcends thoughts, feelings, and images, in touch with the senses, and at ease in the world of ritual and symbol.

The Non-dual Experience

A change in consciousness that comes about as a result of the awakening of one's intuitive faculties is known as the experience of non-duality. Non-duality is also a consequence of growth in inner freedom. As one becomes progressively freed from the false self (see chapter two) with its paralyzing fears, excessive needs, and compulsions, one enters into a purer form of being. The experience of the true self in its fullness is close union with God, the source of all that is.

This insight on non-duality comes to us from the East, from India. It is an experience of pure consciousness, a consciousness beyond the boundaries of time and space. It is a consciousness in which the duality of subject and object has been transcended. Non-duality has to do with cosmic unity. "It is known not by argument and reasoning, not by any activity of the senses or the rational mind, but by an immediate experience of a person's spirit."[15] Therefore, it is not a theory but rather something that happens to us.

One day, in the afternoon, I was sitting on a hillside with a friend of mine. We were sharing our spiritual journeys with one another. Before us lay a beautiful valley and other hills beyond. Sheep and cows grazed on pastures in the valley. Tall trees covered the distant hills. It was a sunny day. My friend was in the midst of sharing her story when suddenly I had an experience of oneness with everything I could see. There was no separation, everything was connected: the ground on which I sat, my friend, the valley, the hills, cows and sheep, trees and sky, all were one in my awareness. The experience did not last long, but it was unforgettable.

A few years ago I gave a weekend retreat on God's presence in nature. I asked the retreatants to take a leisurely walk and simply look and listen without analyzing what they saw and heard. The retreat took place in the mountains so there were plenty of places to stroll. When this time of contemplation-in-nature was over, the retreatants and I gathered together to share our experiences. One man described how he stood next to a large tree. The sun was shining on his face. It was so peaceful, he recounted, that he leaned against the tree to relax. After a while he glanced down and noticed that the rays of the sun which covered his arm and side were also touching part of the tree. The remainder of the tree and the rest of his body were in shadow. Suddenly he had the strange sensation that his arm and the tree were one. He had never had such an experience before. It was a momentary glimpse into the unity of all things.

Both my awareness of being connected to everything around me and the retreatant's experience of oneness between his arm and the tree are experiences of non-duality.

In non-duality "one knows that one is just by actually being."[16] (Recall my experience of the silent mind that I described in chapter four.) There is no object, only subjects. We ask, "How can this be?" The rational mind cannot grasp this. Bede Griffiths writes:

> The rational mind can only work through the senses and discover an "object" of thought. Even the most abstract thought is conditioned by this distinction between subject and object.... This is the limitation of the rational mind. It remains imprisoned in the categories of an objective world.[17]

Enter once again, the value of intuition. Bede Griffiths continues:

> In all religious traditions, Hindu, Buddhist, Muslim, and Christian, it has been recognized that there is a knowledge above reason, a knowledge which is not derived from the senses and is not determined by the categories of rational thought.[18]

In the realm of non-duality there are no boundaries. When one reaches such a state of consciousness in one's prayer, one is in the experience of pure "I Am," communing with God "Who Is." One has progressed from "I-It," relating to God as an object, to "I-Thou," relating to God as person, to "I-I," or "subject-subject coinherence."[19] "I-I" is the ultimate relation. It is what Beatrice Bruteau calls "a co-incidence of two subjects." She explains:

> This "I-I" is not a face-to-face encounter. This is a

co-incidence of two subjects, both facing the same way, so to speak. Each has entered so perfectly into each that it is not right to say "other" any more. Each sees through each's eyes and feels through each's heart, enters into a confluence with each's action. There is no sense of separation, of outside-ness; each is totally inside each.[20]

This is putting on the mind and heart of Christ.

We can come to a greater appreciation of the principle of non-duality in our prayer by using the prayer of imagination. We saw in chapter three how imaginative prayer takes us into a scene from Jesus' life. First we picture ourselves in the scene as a spectator, perhaps as one of the crowd, then as the person who seeks healing if this is the theme of the passage. There is another person we can identify ourself with: Jesus. We can see this in the story of the leper who approached Jesus in search of a cure (Mark 1:40-42). He addressed Jesus, "If you want to, you can make me clean." Jesus responded by stretching out his hand, touching the leper, and saying as he did so: "I do want to. Be clean!" The man was cured immediately. When we identify with Jesus in this scene we look at the leper through Jesus' eyes, we feel with his heart compassion for the man, and we experience the effect of God's healing power as the leprosy vanishes before our very eyes. We have become one with Christ. The closer we come to God in our spiritual journey the more deeply we know ourself as united with Christ and the more we enter into an "I-I" relationship with Christ.

If these reflections on the experience of non-duality seem out of reach to the ordinary person, consider the following account of a prayer experience by a homemaker and mother of two small children:

I went to pray one morning and sat on a chair in our living room. I tried to picture where Jesus was in the room. I knew he was somehow there. I asked him to reveal himself to me. Then, in my imagination, I saw him standing in front of me. I asked him to tell me how he is always with me. He turned around and sat down in me. He said, "I am not around you, I am in you."

This is an "I-I" experience, what Beatrice Bruteau calls, a co-incidence of two subjects.

I must confess, when I first began reading about non-duality I encountered a lot of resistance within myself. It seemed that the authors were saying that the more in union one becomes with God the less one is oneself, that one is absorbed into the divine. I especially found this slant toward "annihilation" of self in books written by some authors from the East. Yet it has been my experience that the closer I come to God the more I am my true self.

One of the gifts of Western culture is the realization of the value of the individual person. There is also the Judeo-Christian insight of Genesis 1:27, that we are made in the image and likeness of God. In addition, my own early personal story involved learning to overcome a poor self-image and feelings of inferiority; a gradual coming to the realization that I have a self and it is good. Thus it was that one day at prayer I found myself reflecting on St. Paul's statement, "I live, not I, it is Christ who lives within me."[21] I asked God to help me understand what this phrase means. An image came to me of two coins. One coin represents Christ, the other, me. In the beginning of my spiritual journey, the coins were far apart. As I grew in prayer and good works, the coins came closer together. As my prayer life deepened still more and as I began to put on the mind and heart of Christ, the two coins started to overlap a bit. As I became more and more my true self, the two coins overlapped more. When I am most my true self, the two coins completely match. What one now sees is one coin: Christ. But when the two coins are turned sideways, one sees that there are still two coins! In other words I do not lose my identity when I become completely united with Christ, who is God, the second person of the Trinity.

It was after I received the image of the two coins that

I found a similar insight from other people. Thomas Merton wrote: "... our true reality in the eyes of God: this reality is 'in God' and 'with God' and belongs entirely to God. Yet of course it is ontologically distinct from God, and in no sense part of the divine nature or absorbed in that nature."[22] From Bede Griffiths I read:

> What becomes of the individual self in this knowledge of the one Self? Does it simply disappear? Here again it is easy to misinterpret the experience of non-duality. There is no doubt that the individual loses all sense of separation from the One and experiences a total unity, but that does not mean that the individual no longer exists. Just as every element in nature is a unique reflection of the one Reality, so every human being is a unique center of consciousness in the universal consciousness. Just as no element in nature is lost in the ultimate reality, so no individual center of consciousness loses its unique character. It participates in the universal consciousness; it knows itself in the unity of the one Being; it discovers itself as a person in the one Person.[23]

And, from *The Divine Milieu*, by Teilhard de Chardin:

> Our God ... pushes to its furthest possible limit the differentiation among the creatures he concentrates within himself. At the peak of their adherence to him, the elect also discover in him the consummation of their individual fulfillment. Christianity alone ... saves ... the essential aspiration of all mysticism: to be *united* (that is, to become the other) while *remaining oneself*.[24]

And, this is not all, according to Teilhard:

> At the heart of the divine *milieu* ... things are transfigured, but from within. They bathe inwardly in light, but, in this incandescence, they retain— this is not strong enough, they exalt—all that is most specific in their attributes. *We can only lose*

ourselves in God by prolonging the most individual characteristics of beings far beyond themselves....[25]

The place within where one experiences non-dual consciousness is known as the "cave of the heart." This term often referred to by the Benedictine, Abhishiktananda, refers to a secret place deep within one's heart.[26] In this deepest part of oneself, one is not only united with God but with all of creation. It is in the cave of the heart that one is most in touch with one's true self. It is here, and in the acts of compassion and love that ones does for others, that the Christian is most closely united with Christ. Beatrice Bruteau reminds us that it is by silence that we come to the secret place of the heart. She describes this process in our prayer:

> I like to think of it (prayer) as a kind of relaxation, or letting go, and sinking in toward the center.... One withdraws from ordinary sense experience, inward toward the vital and emotional feelings; withdrawing from them, one sinks into the memory and the mind; concentrating inward from that, one focuses attention as intuitive insight, within which is the deep sense of appreciation of value, devotion and dedication, and joy in existence, at the very heart of which is the sheer awareness of existence itself.[27]

It is in the cave of the heart that one is most free. Here the emotional wounds of the past lose their sting, pride is lost in self-surrender, and the cup of true self-love is overflowing. This experience is not for a chosen few. Writes Abhishiktananda:

> Yet it is not only monks or cloistered nuns who are called to live face to face with this Presence. All the baptized, indeed every child of God who lives on earth, has his or her dwelling in the bosom of that glory.[28]

A person who has reached this level of inner freedom does not engage in bizarre or eccentric behavior as a result of his or her close union with God. Rather, as Beatrice Bruteau points out:

> Ordinary life is "back," so to speak, in all its ordinariness, and yet transformed from the very bottom of its reality, up. One is not lost in some strange ecstatic state of consciousness, or producing peculiar phenomena, or making a spectacle of oneself in any way. One is doing everything naturally, living out one's true nature.[29]

Moreover, Thomas Keating writes:

> When the presence of God emerges from our inmost being into our faculties, whether we walk down the street or drink a cup of soup, divine life is pouring into the world. The effectiveness of every action depends on the source from which it springs.... If it is coming out of a person who is immersed in God, it is extremely effective.[30]

Six

The Dark Nights

I have come into the world as light, so that
everyone who believes in me should not remain in
the darkness.

—John 12:46

Intrinsic to the spiritual journey and to a life of inner
freedom are two experiences of purification. These two
experiences come under the heading of the dark night, a
term used by St. John of the Cross to describe part of his
pilgrimage to union with God.[1] Many authors have shared
their insight into these passages of purification. What I
wish to do is describe what are known as "the dark night
of sense" and "the dark night of the spirit," and then share
what I have learned from my own journey.

"Night in John of the Cross," writes Sister Constance
Fitzgerald, "is the progressive purification and transfor-
mation of the human person *through* what we cherish or
desire and through what gives us security and support."[2]
It is a passage, through detachment, to a deeper love of
God. It is the way we must go if we wish total union with
God.

The dark night of sense, the first part of what John
of the Cross called "the dark night of the soul," introduces
a person into the state of contemplation. It is, "the purification of the exterior and interior senses,"[3] which serves to
"accommodate sense to spirit by removing the *actual* imperfections of our outer and inner (memory, understanding, imagination) senses."[4] This is the experience of
the silent mind that I described in chapter four: during a

three-day span on an eight-day retreat all thoughts, feelings, and memory were removed from my consciousness as I sat in prayer in complete silence. The reader may wish to re-read this section of chapter four before proceeding.

The dark night of the spirit is a second important transition phase in the life of faith. In this night God leads the person to the state of divine union. This night is, in Thomas Merton's words, "a deeper and more terrible night," than the night of sense, "a hell of mercy." In this time of darkness and trial, "people experience their own nothingness in a spirit of surrender to God."[5] The dark night of the spirit is when God removes one's *habitual* imperfections. John of the Cross explains these imperfections as, "the imperfect affections and habits still remaining like roots in the spirit" after the dark night of sense, "for the sensory purgation could not reach the spirit."[6] Thomas Merton explains the difference between the two nights:

> In the dark night of sense, the exterior self is purified and to a great extent, though not completely, destroyed. But in the dark night of the spirit even the interior person is purified. These two nights are spiritual deaths. In the first, the exterior person "dies" to rise and become the inner person. In the second the interior person dies and rises so completely united to God that the two are one and there remains no division between them except the metaphysical distinction of natures.[7]

The two dark nights are characterized by a loss of control and an experience of powerlessness. In these two levels of purification, "the Spirit of God is calling us beyond ourselves, beyond where we are, into transcendence."[8] We cannot go this way on our own; in this way our humanity limits us. But this is the path to personal wholeness and holiness. This is the journey to the true self.

Both nights are death experiences, but each is a dying in order to rise to new life. Constance Fitzgerald writes:

If we could see the underside of this death, we would realize it is already resurrection. Since we are not educated for darkness, however, we see this experience, because of the shape it takes, as a sign of *death*. Dark night is instead a sign of *life*, of growth, of development in our relationship with God, in our best human relationships, and in our societal life. It is a sign to move on in hope to a new vision, a new experience.[9]

Hidden in darkness are the seeds of new life. Jesus on the cross, in his own dark night of the spirit, cried out with anguish, "My God, my God, why have you forsaken me?" (Mark 15:34, *NAB*). Just before he died, he uttered a loud cry and said, "Father! In your hands I place my spirit!" (Luke 23:46), teaching us in his last words what our disposition must be as well: total surrender and total trust. Through his death came resurrection.

A common temptation as one enters the dark night of the soul is to blame oneself for the aridity one experiences in prayer. A wise spiritual guide will allay this fear by pointing out that "it is an integral part of the development of prayer."[10] Writes Thomas Green:

> The experience of darkness or dryness, then, becomes more and more the normal, constant pattern of our prayer. John of the Cross tells us that this is not a sign of failure or regression; contrary to our natural way of judging things, it is a good and healthy sign of real interior growth.[11]

In the dark night God seems far away, sometimes gone completely. God is not really absent, it just seems that way because we are in darkness. John of the Cross helped us to understand that this state is caused by an excess of light. Though we cannot do anything about the darkness we are in, except live it out in faith, an important attitude to nourish is patience. We can pray for patient endurance.

St. Ignatius of Loyola, in his *Spiritual Exercises* (a classic retreat manual that sprang from the mystical experiences and the spiritual principles with which God gifted him), suggests that when one is in a period of darkness (what Ignatius called, desolation[12]) one should not make or change a decision. Here is a modern translation of the appropriate text:

When we find ourselves weighed down by a certain desolation, we should not try to change a previous decision or to come to a new decision. The reason is that in desolation the evil spirit is making an attempt to obstruct the good direction of our life or to change it, and so we would be thwarted from the gentle lead of God, and what is more conducive to our own salvation. As a result, at a time of desolation, we hold fast to the decision which guided us during the time before the desolation came on us.[13]

This is important advice because when we are in the darkness our only desire is to find a way out. For, in the dark night it is not just our prayer that has gone dry, "life is dry, relationship is dry, ministry is dry."[14] We will grab at any straw, whether in reality it is good for us or not—overeat, get drunk, smoke marijuana, go on a shopping spree, seek affection in inappropriate ways, and so forth. No matter what escapes we use to try to fill the inner emptiness, end the feelings of isolation and loneliness, or get relief from the experience of weakness, the darkness remains.

Souls do not get satisfaction or consolation from the things of God (and) they do not get any out of creatures either. Since God puts a soul in this dark night in order to dry up and purge its sensory appetite, he does not allow it to find sweetness or delight in anything.[15]

However, sometimes the temptation is strong to seek any kind of relief. There is even a kind of false reasoning that can enter our consciousness, indicating that deliverance from the pain is only a distraction away.

About this trial, Constance Fitzgerald writes:

> It is in the throes of this crisis that people abandon God and prayer, a marriage, a friend, a ministry, a community, a church, and forfeit forever the new vision, the genuine hope, the maturity of love and loyalty, dedication and mutuality, that is on the other side of darkness and hopelessness.[16]

When in the dark night, we need to positively cooperate with the work of the Holy Spirit in us by embracing the darkness. Perhaps we need to ask God for freedom from the need to be in control, for, basically, this is what the frantic search for palliatives is all about: feeling out of control. The disposition required in the dark night is surrender, a spiritual free-fall into the loving arms of our God. The following poem, by Ken Eckel, eloquently portrays the habit of mind that leads to an acceptance of our state.

A LEAP INTO THE UNKNOWN

Lord, as you will,
Grant me a faith
That goes beyond
My understanding.

Lord, though I
Cannot even dream
Of what I am asking ...
Though I cannot conceive
Of what you
May have in store ...
This soul of
Your creation
Surrenders.

You Lord,
Be the light
Of my new wisdom.
Take me where
You will.

Then
Use me
To your
Delight.
Amen.[17]

There is something else which can cause confusion when one is in a dark night. Sometimes we are not sure if we are experiencing desolation or depression. The symptoms are similar in both cases. In an excellent article called, "Depression or Dark Night?" Maria Edwards explains that the sense of loss experienced in the beginning stages of the dark night is similar to that which people who are depressed feel.[18] The same symptoms—sadness over the death of a loved one, loss of one's self-esteem or one's sense of security—that often result in depression can be present in the dark night though from a different cause. In the dark night it is the Lord who seems to have vanished, the loss of being in control in one's life and prayer can lead to a lessening of self-esteem, and the experience of powerlessness in this state of unknowing can bring on a profound sense of insecurity.

In her article, Maria Edwards relates some of the differences between primary depression and dark night experiences that have been noted by the psychologist Gerald May.

1. Dark night experiences are usually not related to loss of effectiveness in life and work, as they are with depression.

2. A sense of humor is retained (although subdued) within the dark night, and it is lost in depression.

3. Compassion for others is deepened in the dark night, while self-absorption is characteristic of depression.

4. While emotional suffering is experienced in the dark night, people eventually come to a graced

acceptance of it. Depressives sense a destructiveness about their emotional pain.

5. Others do not feel annoyed or frustrated with people in the dark night, because they are placing their pain before God. Most depressives take no action about their pain and often burden others with it continuously. This causes others to become frustrated with depressives.[19]

I have found the insights of Edwards and May to be of great assistance in my experiences of darkness. At such times it is easy to be misled as to what is happening in one's life and one's prayer, and why.

My own experience of the dark night of the spirit occurred a year to the month after I went through the dark night of sense. As I explained earlier in this chapter, the latter took place while I was on an eight-day retreat; I was staying in a mountain cabin about an hour's drive from San Diego, where I live. The country I was staying in when the second level of purification happened is in itself an experience of darkness: South Africa. This was my second visit to South Africa; I had been there two years previously to give workshops on the social mission of the church. I had returned to learn more about the effects of apartheid on all the people, blacks and whites. This trip was part of a year-long sabbatical, during which I studied and experienced different forms of prayer and a number of situations where there is an absence of social justice. I kept a journal throughout the year. It is from this source that I am able, now, to share what happened and what I learned from a personal experience of the dark night of the spirit. Obviously, one does not have to go to another land to have this trial; it comes whenever and wherever God wishes.

About a week before the darkness descended, while I was celebrating Mass one morning, a line from one of the prayers caught my attention, "Pray continually and never lose heart." I was staying in Johannesburg at the time and had been in South Africa for a week. The lack of equality between blacks and whites was evident everywhere, from segregated public facilities to the great disparity that exists between rich and poor. As had happened on my first trip to this country, I had a sense of the evil that is present in a system like apartheid except this visit the feelings were more intense. A passage from the letter to the Ephesians came to mind, which was to have personal as well as social implications.

> Finally, build up your strength in union with the Lord and by means of his mighty power. Put on all the armor that God gives you, so that you will be able to stand up against the Devil's evil tricks. For we are not fighting against human beings but against the wicked spiritual forces in the heavenly world, the rulers, authorities, and cosmic powers of this dark age. So put on God's armor now! Then when the evil day comes, you will be able to resist the enemy's attacks; and after fighting to the end, you will still hold your ground.... Do all this in prayer, asking for God's help. Pray on every occasion, as the Spirit leads (Ephesians 6:10-13, 18).

I prayed to God for extra energy and strength. I asked that the power of the resurrection flow freely within me. I reaffirmed my belief in the unconditional and everlasting love of God, for myself and all people. I begged the Holy Spirit for greater courage and for the gift of hope.

The day I left Johannesburg to begin a bus trip to various parts of the country, another prayer at Mass caught my eye, "May the humanity of Christ give us courage in our weakness." It was the feast of the Presentation of the Blessed Virgin Mary and I took advantage of the situation by praying, "May the total trust of the Virgin Mary in your power, God, increase my trust in you."

The first stop on my travel itinerary was a Jesuit mission parish, located in a rural area called Elandskop. It is a pretty part of the country composed mostly of farms. It was here, in this quiet pastoral setting, that I entered the dark night of the spirit.

I did not fully realize that I was in a dark night until after the experience. As I look back now, seven years later, I see how important the week previous to the beginning of the darkness was. God was preparing me for this period of purification with meaningful prayers at Mass, the passage from Ephesians, and what was to be the last sign of hope before the trial began, a rainbow. I did not have my camera with me when the rainbow appeared. That I could not capture the moment on film caused me to feel some disappointment until the following words came to my consciousness, "Some things are just for you." With this message came a strong sense of God's presence.[20]

The next eight days were characterized by a loss of appetite, a general feeling of weakness in my body, aches and pains that had no discernible cause, and a darkness of spirit. At times I was besieged with thoughts that my physical discomforts were the result of an amoeba in my system. This reasoning caused a lot of confusion and now reminds me of those who cannot decide if it is depression or a dark night that they are experiencing. When I said, "No," to this line of thought, I felt at peace, though still in a darkness within. I remembered, too, previous times when physical discomfort had accompanied changes in my prayer life. (This makes sense once we realize that spirituality is holistic, that it affects every aspect of who we are; the dying that goes on in the dark night affects body, mind, and spirit.) I asked God for freedom from concern about my body. There was a strong temptation to flee the darkness and physical pain by taking medication.

In the middle of the night of the third day after the severe darkness began, I was awakened by a strong pain in the lower half of my stomach. Mentally and spiritually, I felt as if I was in a train tunnel with no light at the other end. I felt I was going to die. It was not just the pain in my stomach that led to this feeling of impending death, there was something else, some intuition that this was about to happen. I remembered the rainbow I had seen a few days earlier. This recollection seemed to bring me some strength. I was able to face the possibility of death and, in doing so, I let go of all I could think of that I treasure. This surrender of all that I hold dear resulted in the stomach pain going away. (Now I understand Constance Fitzgerald's insight into John of the Cross' use of the word, *"night"*: the progressive purification and transformation … *through* what we cherish or desire and through what give us security and support.) I realized what I cherish most is friends; names of friends came to mind during this time of prayer and I let each one go.

The following morning, when I awakened, I was surprised to still be alive, so strong had the thought of dying been during the night.

Awakening in the middle of the night became a pattern during the eight-day trial. In the fourth night, after sleeping fine for about three hours, I woke up. I was feeling bad in body and spirit again. I wondered if I should cut short my trip to South Africa in order to recuperate in more familiar surroundings. I prayed to know God's will and I asked God for the freedom to do what he wanted. I decided to put off making a decision on this for a few days. (Perhaps, in my subconscious, I remembered St. Ignatius' advice not to change a decision when in desolation.) Words from my prayer of the previous week came back to me: "Draw your strength from the Lord and his mighty power." "Never lose heart." I used the freedom-prayer a lot that night, especially in relation to the various unexplainable aches and pains I felt in my body. I asked God for freedom from the need to know the cause of my not feeling well, so that I would not feel anxious about the unwellness. At some point I began to think about the many men, women, and children who were in jail in South Africa. At that time the state of emergency was in effect. They were being held in detention without trial because of their stand against apartheid. I felt in solidarity with them in my experience of powerlessness. The idea of this period of darkness being like what I would experience if I were in jail, came clearly to me. (Now I have Gerald May's fifth point to reflect back with. Instead of self-absorption completely capturing my attention, compassion for others deepened in my dark night of the spirit.)

During the eight days I had a lack of desire to do anything constructive, no will to do anything. However, I did manage to accomplish small tasks: I was able to wash my clothes, read a novel, and exercise a bit. I had to push myself to eat, as I did not feel like taking in food.

The Jesuits at the mission were very supportive— one of the few rays of hope that came to me during this time.

Because the experience of the dark night affected every part of my being, I was not able to pray the centering prayer that I had become accustomed to; it was just too painful to simply sit in the quiet. Instead, I wrote out what I was feeling. The following is an example of how I prayed.

> Lord, you know how I feel today
> and how I felt last night.
> There is a strong feeling of grief
> in the center of my chest.
> I pray for patient endurance.
> I pray to let go of any plans I had
> for these days in Elandskop.
> Please give me your strength,
> I rely on your strength.
> Increase in me confidence in my ability
> to carry this cross
> for as long as you wish me to carry it.
> Help me to keep my eyes fixed firmly
> on the resurrection.
> May I believe ever more deeply
> that life will win over death,
> that your truth will conquer all lies and injustice.
> Stimulate and expand my hope
> in you,
> in your love,
> in your power,
> in my salvation,

and the salvation of this country.
Give me the courage of faith
    and ultimate trust in you.
I believe you are upholding me today
    as you have since I arrived in South Africa,
    as you have done throughout my life.
Out of this trial may I become
    a more compassionate person
    toward all those I come in contact with.
Make me courageous for justice
    and compassionate in love.
Please give me a joyful, peaceful, willingness
    to suffer for you,
    to suffer and die in defense of your name,
    and for the dignity of your children.
Amen.

On the fifth day, my appetite began improving. In addition, the desire to do things started to return, although I still did not have the energy to accomplish them. The following morning I went with the pastor to visit a woman who was dying. Sitting with her, in her home, I knew with my whole heart how she felt as she watched her life ebbing away, such was the intensity of what I had just been through myself. This was the first day since the darkness began that I had the energy to go to Mass. The readings were about God's power, about hope, and about eternal salvation. Especially moving for me were these words from the responsorial psalm refrain: "They are happy, whose strength is in you. They walk with growing strength" (Psalm 84). The following passage from the prophet Isaiah was in the song we sang during Mass; it moved me to tears.

Don't you know? Haven't you heard?
The LORD is the everlasting God;
    [the Lord] created all the world.
[The Lord] never grows tired or weary.
    No one understands [God's] thoughts.

[The Lord] strengthens those who are weak and
tired.
Even those who are young grow weak;
    young men [and women] can fall exhausted.
But those who trust in the LORD for help
    will find their strength renewed.
They will rise on wings like eagles;
    they will run and not get weary;
    they will walk and not grow weak (Isaiah 40:28-31).

Part of my pain, I had realized at Mass that day, was the
absence—except for the rainbow—of consoling thoughts
since the dark night began. Consequently, the two passages from the Old Testament mentioned above were like
"shafts of light" penetrating the darkness.

The seventh and eighth days saw a gradual returning of my physical strength. I began taking walks in the
countryside. I was tempted, now and then, to think that
what I had been through was caused by a parasite. However, as before when I entertained such thoughts, I was
filled with anxiety and confusion. When I held to the
conviction that I had been through some form of dark
night, I felt at peace. I used St. Ignatius' rule for discernment of spirits to keep myself on track: if the thought
brings anxiety, worry, confusion, the source is the bad
spirit; if peace it is the good spirit who is the originator.[21]
My efforts were rewarded on the evening of the seventh
day when I read the following words from an article by
Thomas Merton that I "happened" to have with me. (His
message was so appropriate to the previous seven days
that it seemed to me more than coincidence that I should
read them.)

In the dark night of the spirit ... the interior person
is purified. In the dark night of sense, the exterior
self "dies" to rise and become the inner person. In
the dark night of the spirit the interior person dies
and rises so completely united to God that the two
are one and there remains no division between

them except the metaphysical distinction of na-
tures.[22]

The darkness lifted on the eighth day, though I was
to feel effects of it for a couple of weeks: a lack of physical
energy at times, a few aches and pains with no discernible
cause, periodic diminishment of desire to do anything,
and occasional periods of darkness in my prayer. My
prayer continued to be one of writing down what I was
feeling, and asking God for what I needed—strength, a
particular freedom, inner peace, greater trust in God, and
more confidence in myself. God spoke to my heart through
scripture passages at Mass. I also found the effects of God's
presence in the depth of compassion I felt for the suffering
people of South Africa.

I left the Jesuit mission at Elandskop on the ninth
day after I had arrived. During the following three weeks,
I traveled by bus throughout the country, stopping for a
few days in different cities. We drove through the Transkei
and the Ciskei, the so-called "homelands" designated by
the white South African government for African people.
These are, in reality, dumping grounds without the fertile
land for agriculture that the white-owned farms have. I
visited some of the black townships in Port Elizabeth and
Cape Town and saw with my own eyes the terrible living
conditions of the people there. I met a white woman who
was in jail for two weeks. She was charged with obstruct-
ing justice: she had stopped a white policeman from beating a black man with a whip! I saw the great disparity of
living conditions between the rich and the poor. In all of
this, I felt the impact of what I was experiencing at a deeper
level within myself than I had before I went through the
dark night of the spirit. God had not only purified my
heart of what I cherished most (friends) during the dark
night, but had also enlarged my heart to take in at a more
profound depth the suffering of people.

I end this personal recollection with a prayer I wrote
on the day before leaving the Jesuit mission in Elandskop.

My heart is wounded.
I languish, waiting for you, God,
to heal me.
I wait on your love
that will return my spirit to me,
a new spirit,
and a new depth of inner peace.
With John of the Cross, I pray,
"Quench thou my griefs,
and let mine eyes behold thee."
Find me.
I am wounded by your love.
I need your love
   to breathe
   to walk and eat
   to laugh and cry
   to do simple actions
   to feel an emotion or
   to think a thought.
Show me that which my wounded heart desires.
Energize me with your loving power.
Amen.

Seven

The Call to Compassion and Justice

> This is what love is: it is not that we have loved
> God, but that [God] loved us and sent [the] Son to
> be the means by which our sins are forgiven. Dear
> friends, if this is how God loved us, then we should
> love one another.
>
> *—1 John 4:10-11*

In the opening chapter of this book we considered the
foundation of our identity: the unconditional love of God.
Then we considered various methods of prayer. Beginning
with the freedom-prayer, we reflected on discursive
prayer, praying the scriptures, using our imagination in
prayer, centering prayer, and the quieter contemplative
prayer. We looked at the different changes in consciousness that come about as a result of our growing union with
God.

   Concern for the wounded in society was never far
from these considerations. Sometimes compassion was
explicit, as in the section on Christ-consciousness; at other
times, it was there in my personal sharings. This is as it
should be. Ladislaus Boros reminds us that prayer is not
a running away from the world, but a deeper embracing
of it. Even the monastic does not enter the monastery to
take refuge from the world. Thomas Merton, who was a
Trappist monk, wrote:

> We do not go into the desert to escape people but
> to learn how to find them; we do not leave them in
> order to have nothing more to do with them, but
> to find out the way to do them the most good.[1]

Each of us is involved to some extent in reaching out to people who are wounded. Perhaps the person, or people, we care about are suffering from economic poverty, perhaps from an addiction or a terminal illness. Possibly our concern is for the unborn and the threat of abortion. Just as we need, periodically, to reflect on the basis of our self-worth—God's love for us—so also it is important to review the *why* of our compassion and concern for social justice. The book of Exodus is where we start.

In Exodus 1:8-14 we read about the life of the early Israelites. They were living in slavery in Egypt where the Egyptians oppressed them cruelly with forced labor. Yet, the more they were oppressed the greater their number became.[2] They cried out to God for help to free them from their oppression.

Into this situation came Moses. One day, while he was tending the flock of his father-in-law, he had an unusual experience. He saw a bush on fire, but the flames were not consuming it. He decided to draw closer to the bush in order to have a better look at this incredible sight.

> When the LORD saw that Moses was coming closer, [God] called to him from the middle of the bush and said, "Moses! Moses!" He answered, "Yes, here I am." God said, "Do not come any closer. Take off your sandals, because you are standing on holy ground. I am the God of your ancestors, the God of Abraham, Isaac, and Jacob." So Moses covered his face, because he was afraid to look at God (Exodus 3:4-6).

Here is a completely different kind of power than the king of Egypt had. For Moses, the sheepherder, this was a religious experience that both startled and, as we shall see, empowered him to do things beyond his wildest imaginings. This was the *call* of Moses. Perhaps our call from God was not as dramatic as the burning bush, but it is the same God who calls us today. Moses' reaction upon hearing the voice was fear, a healthy response to such a mysterious encounter. Then God said to Moses:

"I have seen how cruelly my people are being treated in Egypt; I have heard them cry out to be rescued from their slave drivers. I know all about their sufferings.... I have indeed heard the cry of my people, and I see how the Egyptians are oppressing them" (Exodus 3:7, 9).

Here is the basis of our compassion: the response of our compassionate God! This is not a God who is uninterested or uninvolved in the plight of those who are in anguish. Our God sees oppression and responds with concern, hears the groanings of a people caught in slavery and determines to do something about it. God continues:

"And so I have come down to rescue [the Israelites] from the Egyptians and to bring them out of Egypt to a fertile and spacious land, one which is rich and fertile" (Exodus 3:8).

Here, too, is the foundation for our commitment to social justice: *it is the nature of God!* Compassion and a passion for the rights of all are essential qualities of God's nature. God is both motive and ultimate source of our preferential option for the poor and for our actions on behalf of those who are oppressed.[3]

In an excellent book on compassion, the authors refer to Jesus' life and the source of his loving and healing care for people.

It was out of his compassion that Jesus' healing emerged. He did not cure to prove, to impress, or to convince. *His cures were the natural expression of his being our God....* The great mystery is not the cures, but the infinite compassion which is their source.[4]

Compassion and a concern for social justice come from the nature of God as seen clearly in Exodus. This is indeed a challenge, for not only are we to hear the cry of those who are suffering in our day but we are also to act for their liberation whenever this is possible. Jesus' instruction, "Be compassionate, as your Father is compassionate" (Luke 6:36, *NAB*), takes us directly to prayer, for without God's help we could never approach this depth of compassion and care.

After expressing concern about the plight of the Israelites, God missioned Moses: "Now I am sending you to the king of Egypt so that you can lead my people out of his country" (Exodus 3:10).

Moses' reaction, "I am nobody. How can I go to the king and bring the Israelites out of Egypt?" (Exodus 3:11), was perfectly understandable. Who was Moses but a shepherd? In addition, he was a fugitive from the court of the king for having killed an Egyptian who was beating a Hebrew (Exodus 2:11-16). His response to God is reminiscent of the prophet Jeremiah when he was called by God: "I don't know how to speak; I am too young" (Jeremiah 1:6). Is not incredulity our reaction too when we feel the nudge of the Spirit to confront some unjust law or system, be it in the church, in business, or in the government, when we are asked to challenge the misuse of power by a modern day king? Like Moses, we are fascinated by the religious experience (for Moses, the burning bush), but the task that often follows such an encounter with God fills us with fear. We cry out: "I am powerless!" "I am helpless!" "I am afraid!" "What will it cost me?" "I do not know enough about the issue!" and so forth. The response of God to Moses' reluctance for the mission is God's answer to us as well: "I will be with you" (Exodus 3:12). God's reassurance to Jeremiah is similar: "Do not be afraid of them, for I will be with you to protect you" (Jeremiah 1:8). Such a message not only reassures, it empowers us to carry out the mission God gives us, even as it enabled both Moses and Jeremiah to accomplish theirs.

Perhaps an experience from my own life will shed further light on this dynamic of empowerment. I mentioned in chapter six, in the section on the dark night of the spirit, that I went to South Africa in 1986 to learn more about the conditions of people living under apartheid. I was in Zambia for a month before I went to South Africa.

(I had been in South Africa two years previously to give workshops on the social mission of the church.) A week before I was to depart from Zambia, the United States government voted to impose economic sanctions on South Africa! I was already fearful about returning since a state of emergency was in effect, rendering the country a police state. As the time approached for me to depart for South Africa, my body started to react. Aches and pains appeared, with no discernible cause. I started to lose my appetite. My enjoyment of community diminished, I felt withdrawn and uncommunicative.

The day before I was to leave Zambia, I went to a priest where I was staying to receive the sacrament of reconciliation. For a penance, he suggested I pray the Magnificat in thanksgiving for all the graces God had given to me thus far on my trip. With this penance in mind, I returned to my room where I opened the Bible in search of Luke 1 and Mary's prayer. I set the Bible down for a moment. When I went to read the passage assigned by my confessor, the Bible was now open to Isaiah 51. I thought, "Fine, but this is not the passage I want." Once again, I went in search of Luke 1, *and*, once again, the Bible opened to Isaiah 51! I looked at the page and read these words:

I, it is I who comfort you.[5]

I felt great relief as I read this sentence. Over and over I read this line and each time the relief seemed to spread through me. After awhile, I looked at the next sentence:

Can you then fear mortal man,
who is human only, to be looked upon as grass....

"No, I do not need to fear people!" I exclaimed to myself with a forcefulness that startled me. Adrenalin coursed through me as I considered the meaning of this verse, and the one that followed it:

And forget the LORD, your maker,
who stretched out the heavens
and laid the foundations of the earth?

"Yes!" I responded, "God's power is greater than anything I will encounter in South Africa!" A new level of confidence started to emerge within me as I pondered this verse of Isaiah.

However, the next line astonished me with the accuracy of its description of the state of my emotions:

All the day you are in constant dread
of the fury of the oppressor....

Talk about naming one's fear! I keenly felt God's presence in the room; it seemed as if God were sitting in the chair opposite me speaking to me and giving me the strength I needed to go back to South Africa. God consoled me even further with the next line:

But when he sets himself to destroy,
what is there of the oppressor's fury?

I could relate to the message here as I recalled the words of many men and women as they faced physical danger from oppressive governments, "They can take away my life, but not my integrity!" Time passed quickly as I prayed these lines of Isaiah 51. After about an hour's reflection on these words (verses 12 and 13), I glanced back to verse 9 and read:

Awake, awake, put on strength,
O arm of the Lord!

By then I was feeling much better, stronger, and at peace in the prospect of leaving for Johannesburg the following day. God had indeed empowered me for whatever trials lay ahead.

A curious thing about this prayerful experience is that I could not remember ever having read this chapter before. In fact, as I sat there marveling at the graces I had just received, I decided to see how it begins. I smiled with further amazement as I read:

Listen to me, you who pursue justice,
who seek the LORD;
Look to the rock from which you were hewn,
to the pit from which you were quarried (Isaiah 51:1).

The next day I boarded the plane and flew to South Africa.

Love, The Essence of Compassion

Let us return to Exodus 3:

> Then the Lord said, "I have seen how cruelly my people are being treated in Egypt; I have heard them cry out to be rescued from their slave drivers. I know all about their sufferings ..." (Exodus 3:7).

To know all about another's suffering involves more than casual contact with the other person(s). I believe that our commitment to compassion and social justice is, basically, about making friends. The oppressed, the wounded, the sick become our friends; we begin to see life through their eyes. We enter into their world and join them in such ordinary activities as sharing a meal together, looking through their family photo album, listening to their story, playing with the children, having a beer, and so forth. We spend quality time with them.

In my own life I have a deeper compassion and understanding for the Mexican family who wants to cross the border into the United States, even illegally, because I have been in many homes in Tijuana and know first hand the terrible effects of poverty: high unemployment, lack of education for the children, diseases which have been practically eradicated on the other side of the border, houses with dirt floors, etc. I now see the border from Tijuana as well as from California. The authors of the book *Compassion* express it this way:

> Compassion asks us to go where it hurts, to enter into places of pain, to share in brokenness, fear, confusion, and anguish. Compassion challenges us to cry out with those in misery, to mourn with those who are lonely, to weep with those in tears. Compassion requires us to be weak with the weak, vulnerable with the vulnerable, and powerless with the powerless.[6]

There is a form of contemplation I sometimes use in Tijuana that leads me to a greater depth of compassion. I sit on the side of a hill in Colonia Esperanza, where the mission church I go to is located. From this vantage point I can see the simple dwellings of the people. There is little vegetation, the roads are unpaved, the small houses are jumbled together, there are outdoor toilet facilities, old abandoned cars sit stranded here and there, clothes are hanging out to dry on makeshift fences, and in the midst of it all children are playing. During this time of reflection, I try not to analyze what I am seeing. I simply want to *be* there, drinking in the scene, letting God speak to my heart through the reality of the poverty.[7]

Who needs our compassion? Obviously, anyone who is suffering—physically, emotionally, or spiritually. However, within the general call to compassion there is a special need today to reach out to those who are economically poor. This is so for two reasons: when we consider the whole world, we learn that two-thirds of the people live in poverty; and, it is in regard to those who are materially poor that our inner resistances are the strongest. In regard to this second reason, we struggle with myths about why people are out of work or on welfare. We think, they could work if they wanted to, they're lazy, they're trying to cheat the government, and so forth. We hesitate to give money to the beggar for fear that the person might not really need it or that the other will take advantage of us.

A few years ago I came upon a very challenging passage from the Book of Sirach (also known as Ecclesiasticus) in the Old Testament. In Sirach 4 we read such admonitions as: "[My child,] don't prevent the poor from making a living, or keep them waiting in their need." "Don't turn your back on a poor person." "Listen to what the poor have to say, and answer them politely" (Sirach 4:1, 5, 8). Perhaps we keep the person "waiting in their need" because of a judgmental attitude on our part. Perhaps we feel guilty when we compare our lifestyle to theirs and so we turn our back to the other. What is required first is an attitude of listening. This attitude has to do with recognizing the other as another human being—my brother or sister in Christ—who is in need. Listening to the homeless man or woman, the street kid, the refugee, and answering them with courtesy, does not necessarily imply giving money to them. In fact, I may decide not to give financial help but that need not prohibit me from a friendly greeting, with eye contact, and a "No thank you today." These are simple acts of love.[8]

It is important to become aware of our resistances toward treating the wounded person as our brother or sister and to bring these obstacles to God for healing. We might use the freedom-prayer, asking God for freedom from the fear of the other (who may be very unlike us in manner of dress, in cleanliness, in state of life) if this is a resistance, or freedom from feelings of guilt as we compare our lifestyle to theirs, that we might love the other in simple ways. Sometimes the situation when we meet the person in need does involve physical danger. In this case, prudence would be required and avoidance of dangerous contact is the action to take.

As I mentioned above, all of those who deserve our attention and compassion are not economically poor. People can be wounded in a variety of ways. When we consider the life of Jesus we notice him reaching out to tax collectors and prostitutes, neither of which were necessarily materially poor, as well as beggars and poor widows. Peter McVerry suggests that Jesus had a preferential concern "for those who were rejected, despised, looked down upon, treated as of little worth, denied a full place in the society of his own time."[9] This definition remains valid today. These are people "who are not, in practice, given equal respect and status in society."[10]

Compassion involves conversion. Jean Vanier writes:

> Compassion is not a passing emotion. It is more than a gesture of tenderness without commitment. To be compassionate is to turn with an open heart towards those who are afflicted. It requires a heart which is understanding and full of goodness, which seeks ways of giving assistance and support.[11]

Occasionally God leads us through an experience of conversion to compassion in the midst of what is already a situation of suffering. Such was the case a few years ago when one of the families in Colonia Esperanza asked me to bring a doctor to their home to find out what was wrong with one of their teen-age daughters. She had been having seizures. The family lived in a two-room, wooden house perched on the side of a hill. Furniture was sparse; the flooring was bare cement. I brought a young Mexican-American doctor, Luis, to see the girl. Her name was Francesca. It was early evening when we arrived at her house. Relatives from across the road gathered with the family as Luis and I entered the house. We were given the only two chairs the family had. There was a gas lamp on the floor; I had brought a flashlight for Luis, there being no electricity in the home. Every person I have brought to the Colonia from the United States has had a conversion experience there. I was fully expecting the same opening of heart to happen to Luis. Although he is of Mexican descent, he is not economically poor. What I had not anticipated was that both of us would experience conversion.

While I was holding the flashlight for Luis as he checked Francesca's eyes, I noticed movement to my side. I turned and saw a young girl being held by her mother. I noticed that she had no motor control, her head and her arms flopped about. I felt a knot in my stomach and I turned away from the sight of her deformity. I realized that I had just done a very unloving action. I asked God to heal me of the repugnance I felt toward this girl. I found myself looking at her again. I reached out my arm toward her. She smiled at me. Her mother saw my arm and released her. Slowly the girl drifted toward me until she was standing next to me, as I sat on the chair. I put my arm around her and drew her to me. We stayed that way until the doctor was finished diagnosing Francesca's illness. As we bade goodbye to the family, I bent down and kissed the young girl on her forehead. I have since learned that the girl's name is Sylvia. Whenever I am in the vicinity of her home,

I go to see her. We are friends. And, Francesca is doing well because, thanks to Luis, she now has the medicine she needs to take care of the seizures.

"To be compassionate is to turn with an open heart towards those who are afflicted," writes Jean Vanier. Sylvia is a reminder to me that conversion to compassion is an ongoing experience and that God's healing presence can come to us in the most unexpected of times. Sylvia's giftedness is, paradoxically, in her helplessness: I who am sound in body and mind am a more compassionate human being because of her. I realize now, too, that her affection and trust is her compassion toward me in what was my affliction, the repugnance I felt when I first saw her.

Intuition, Compassion, and Justice

In chapter five, we considered intuitive knowledge and some of its characteristics: it is a matter of *being* rather than of *doing*, it is receptive rather than aggressive, it involves listening at a deep level, and it relates well to symbols, gestures, and ritual. Intuition is real knowledge. We learned from Frances Vaughan that intuition allows us to draw on our vast storehouse of unconscious knowledge.[12] Bede Griffiths helped us to understand that when we penetrate beyond the rational mind we discover a deeper self.[13] We saw how intimately connected are intuition and contemplation. Now we need to ask how this rich resource of the mind is related to our actions of compassion and social justice.

A book that has been especially helpful to me in understanding the role of intuition in service is called *How Can I Help?* by Ram Dass and Paul Gorman. I would like to draw especially from chapter four, "The Listening Mind." The authors remind us that how well we serve others depends upon our state of mind. When our mind is agitated, for example, it is hard to listen to what someone else is saying. When our mind is quiet we can be more receptive, even to stories of loss and of tragedy.

The authors are quick to point out what writers on

the science of the brain maintain—that there is more to the mind than reason alone. There is the experience of awareness itself. They write:

> Moreover, there is something we frequently experience—perhaps we can call it intuitive awareness—that links us most intimately to the universe and, in allegiance with the heart, binds us together in generosity and compassion.... This resource of awareness can give us access to deeper power, power to help and heal.[14]

There are numerous blocks to this kind of awareness. Allow me to describe four we frequently experience.

First, there is the busy, analytical, mind: while supposedly listening to someone tell me their problem, I am two steps ahead just waiting for them to be quiet so I can give them the answer! Instead of being present to the other person, I am in my own thoughts. This is far from what is known as "the fasting of the heart."[15] Fasting of the heart means hearing with one's spirit. This kind of listening demands an emptying of one's faculties so that listening with one's whole being is made possible. Fasting of the heart frees us from the tyranny of the busy mind and leads to inner unity.

A second block is a judgmental attitude toward the other person. I make a moral judgment before I know all the facts. Inwardly I have dismissed the person as he or she actually is—a person of value. Karen Jaenke writes that judgmentalism is actually a defense mechanism, which protects the judger from the other, who is viewed as inferior or disgusting. The need to judge, she explains, arises from one's own sense of insecurity. She quotes Morton Kelsey:

> Before there can be any real love, one must find out what the other person is like. One has to become aware, conscious of the person's true being, in order to love that very person and not some image of one's own that one projects upon the other....

And probably the surest way of finding out the difference is by listening to the other person....[16]

Once I have judged the other, I can no longer hear what he or she is really saying. My mind is closed.

A third obstacle to intuitive awareness is exhaustion. I am completely worn-out in helping others yet I keep trying to respond to people's needs. Perhaps I have a compulsion to appear responsible or have an unresolved need to be needed. I may believe that the good Christian is one who is always available to everyone regardless of his or her own need for rest. I may need to pray for the freedom to take time off. St. Paul counsels, "The relief of others ought not to impoverish you..." (2 Corinthians 8:13, *NAB*). Not only is my well-being harmed by over-work, I can do serious damage to the person seeking assistance when I am responding from an exhausted state.[17]

Fourth, I may fancy myself as superior to the other person or group. *I* know what is best for them. With this kind of attitude, I am not able to hear what others can do to help themselves, what strengths they have. In terms of working with people who are caught in the trap of poverty, this disposition leads to an unhealthy dependence on the giver. An excellent response to this kind of mindset is the philosophy of Servol (Service Volunteered for All), an organization that has its origins in Trinidad.[18] Servol was founded to empower those who are materially poor.

The teaching of Servol contains three steps:

1. In reaching out to help disadvantaged people, one should base one's approach on a *philosophy of ignorance*. This means that one should never presume to know what the needs of the people are; one asks the people what they need and what kind of help they are seeking.

2. The next step is that of *attentive listening*: a careful listening to what the people say. This form of respect comes from the conviction that the voice of the people is the most important element in their own development.

3. After having asked the people what they need and

having adopted an attitude of listening, one is permitted to interfere in their lives through a process of *respectful intervention*. Implied here is a consciousness that we both have a lot to learn from dialogue, and that we will both emerge richer from the experience.

Ram Dass and Paul Gorman offer the term "spacious awareness" to describe the ideal helping mind. Like the prayer of contemplation, which involves detachment from thoughts, spacious awareness occurs when we let go of identifying with each thought that comes into our consciousness as we seek to help someone. In this state: "We can remain quiet and choose which thoughts we wish to attend to. And we can remain aware *behind* all these thoughts, in a state that offers an entirely new level of openness and insight."[19] This awareness not only helps us to hear what the other person is really saying, it allows us to hear whatever it is that is going on inside *us*: our skills and our needs, our limits and our strengths. And, "the more deeply we listen, the more we attune ourselves to the root of suffering and the means to help alleviate it."[20] I would add to these benefits that the quieter our mind the more clearly we are able to discern God's suggestions as to approach and response to the one in need. And, the more effective we can be as a channel of God's healing grace. Other positive aspects of a listening mind are: openness, humility, patience, sensitivity, and presence.

A stance of openness enables us to enter into the experience of someone else by listening to their story. In the 1960s I worked in the African-American community in San Francisco. I began ministry there by going door-to-door and asking people a simple question: What is it like to be black and live in San Francisco? The responses to this inquiry opened my mind and my heart to the African-American struggle in the United States as I heard personal stories of discrimination and exclusion. Gradually I began to see organizations and institutions from the point of view of a people that had been systematically denied full access to them, something that had been foreign to my own experience.

When we are willing to enter into a situation in which we do not have all the answers and, in fact, feel insecure at times, yet we stay with the people, we are practicing humility. Visiting someone who is terminally ill, serving in another culture where we are not fluent in the language, choosing to live in an economically poor neighborhood or confronting an unjust government are activities that lead us to feelings of helplessness and powerlessness. This experience of our own weaknesses puts us into solidarity with all other human beings, for we all suffer brokenness and we are all in need of healing.[21]

Patience means waiting for the right solution to our present problem. It takes discipline. It involves listening at a deep level. It means trusting in the intuitive mind, that vast storehouse of knowledge connected to the individual and collective unconscious. Someone who was a genius at this kind of listening-waiting was Mahatma Gandhi. Consider the following story from his life.

> Once when Gandhi's supporters were stymied as to what action to take next, Gandhi went off to listen. He listened for three months, much to the impatience of his supporters, and then he set off on the Salt March. He'd heard what this could mean to the Indian "salt of the earth." He'd heard how close salt was to their daily lives, how it came from the sea itself, nature's provision, and yet was taxed by the British. He'd heard that the masses would be moved by so simple a gesture as claiming the salt of God's sea. He'd heard that the British were vulnerable, public opinion at home was turning, labor unions were already sympathetic to the struggle. He'd heard that if he set out, alone or with a few followers, people would join, and joyfully. He'd heard that all he had to do was to start walking.... And people started following, more and more. And when they arrived at the sea, Gandhi bathed and purified himself, then took a handful of salt from the beach and just held it up.

Within one month, seventy thousand Indians had been jailed for mining their own salt, with more ready to follow their example and no room in the jails. Gandhi had heard that there would be nothing for the British to do except back down, and they did. Just the right action, at just the right time, coming from the mind "harmonized with the activities of all things in nature."[22]

Increased sensitivity to the needs of others is a direct result of the quiet mind. Such was the case of Mary at the wedding in Cana (John 2:1-10). She notices that the wine has run out and she is sensitive to the embarrassment of her hosts. She then brings this unfortunate predicament to the attention of her son. She models for us the lesson of the third chapter of Exodus: true compassion leads to some kind of action.

Compassion is often expressed in a ministry of presence. In chapter four we reflected on the present moment as it relates to our prayer. How, we might ask, is presence part of our service? Karen Jaenke shares her experience of working with those who have AIDS.

AIDS confronts us with an enormous sense of helplessness. Most of us are result-oriented, like to see tangibles, need external confirmation. AIDS gives very little of that.... If one is to endure in this ministry, it must be grounded on some other basis.... For me, this basis is presence. I refer to an accepting presence, also called unconditional love.[23]

An "accepting presence" is especially difficult when the one who is suffering is difficult to look at because of their disfigurement. Mother Teresa of Calcutta encourages us to minister to Christ "in all his distressing disguises." During Mass one day she told her sisters, "When you touch the poor you are touching the Body of Christ."[24]

An accepting presence is especially heartbreaking when the one in pain is someone close to us, perhaps even a member of our own family. We can look to Mary again for inspiration. Jean Vanier describes her role at the foot of the cross: "She knew that her son's hour had come. She was there, not to remove his pain, but to help him to live it to the full, to support and encourage him so that the work of the Father might be accomplished."[25] To accomplish her ministry of presence she had to get beyond yet not deny her own suffering at the sight of her son in agony.

Jesus teaches us about having an accepting presence in a variety of ways. Firstly, he *noticed* the plight of the poor and the sick. He was not afraid to look at their disfigurement. Secondly, he was *approachable*. People with all kinds of ailments came to him. These were men, women, and children who were ostracized from the main community, people who were embarrassed about their problem. We do not disclose what we feel shame about to another unless we trust them. In the gospels we learn a lot about the kind of person Jesus was by the kind of personal traumas people shared with him: the man with leprosy, the woman with the hemorrhage, a blind beggar, the woman who was badly stooped because she had been possessed by a bad spirit for eighteen years, to name just a few. In Jesus, the poor and the sick found nonjudgmental compassion. In Jesus, they found a friend. Even the sinner found his or her dignity intact after being in his company (see Luke 7:36-50, John 8:1-11).

Thirdly, Jesus *touched* the wounded as he healed them. This means he became personally involved with each person; this was not impersonal contact. "After sunset all who had friends who were sick with various diseases brought them to Jesus; he placed his hands on every one of them and healed them all" (Luke 4:40). Gesture is an important aspect of the intuitive; being in touch with one's body, one's senses, and being free to express one's feelings of compassion to the other.

Even in his confrontations with the scribes and the Pharisees, Jesus utilized his intuitive faculties. He tried many ways to reach them, to get them to conversion. First he invited them to re-think their positions. Then he told them parables to open their minds and their hearts. When neither of these approaches bore fruit, he discerned and chose another method—he confronted them with strong language:

> "How terrible for you, teachers of the Law and Pharisees! You hypocrites! You give to God one tenth even of the seasoning herbs, such as mint, dill, and cumin, but you neglect to obey the really important teachings of the Law, such as justice and mercy and honesty. These you should practice, without neglecting the others" (Matthew 23:23).

Jesus instructed his disciples to "shake the dust off your feet" (Mark 6:11) if any place would not receive them, the final discernment if the people were hardened in their hearts.

Finally, Jesus knew when it was time to take a rest from the demands of the ministry.

> The apostles returned and met with Jesus, and told him all they had done and taught. There were so many people coming and going that Jesus and his disciples didn't even have time to eat. So he said to them, "Let us go off by ourselves to some place where we will be alone and you can rest a while" (Mark 6:30-31).

Jesus encourages us to do the same, to take time out to pray and to play. The ministry of compassion and social justice is demanding. We cannot do it alone and we are not able to carry it through to completion without time for ourselves. Jesus says to us:

> "Come to me, all of you who are tired from carrying heavy loads, and I will give you rest. Take my yoke and put it on you, and learn from me, because I am gentle and humble in spirit; and you will find rest" (Matthew 11:28-29).

Eight

Compassion for the Earth

Praise the LORD from the earth,
sea monsters and all ocean depths;
lightning and hail, snow and clouds,
strong winds that obey [God's] command.
Praise [God,] hills and mountains,
fruit trees and forests;
all animals, tame and wild,
reptiles and birds.

—Psalm 148:7-10

We read in chapter one that God invites us to a deeper appreciation of our value as human beings. We are to see ourselves through the eyes of God: loved unconditionally, wonderfully made, endlessly treasured. In chapter seven, we considered the call from God to reach beyond ourselves, in love, to other people, especially the wounded of society. St. John reminds us of this double obligation of love in his first letter:

Dear friends, if this is how God loved us,
then we should love one another (1 John 4:11).

Recently, many of us have come to realize that our love must extend to all of creation—to animals and insects, rocks and mountains, rivers and seas, flowers and trees, earth and sky—everything that God has created. Some of us have come to this awareness by means of our prayer. Reflecting on the beauty of nature, we have become saddened by the abuse of it by human beings. Others have been converted to a greater sensitivity for the planet through social analysis. Such assaults on nature as deforestation, the use of harmful pesticides, air and water pollution, species extinction, and toxic waste have convinced us that there are threats to the very *integrity* of creation.

To reverse this process of environmental abuse we need concrete, practical action, in both local and global arenas. However, as Sean McDonagh points out in his insightful book, *To Care for the Earth*, a deep spiritual change must also take place within every person.[1] We need to develop an eco-spirituality to counteract eco-destruction.

St. Francis of Assisi

In 1979 Pope John Paul II proclaimed St. Francis of Assisi heavenly patron of ecology. In his 1990 Peace Day message, the Pope wrote, "Francis ... offers Christians an example of genuine and deep respect for the integrity of creation."[2] Franciscan Father Louis Vitale reminds us how St. Francis, in his time, heard the message of God's goodness, of creation's interdependence and of humanity's responsibility toward it.[3] Francis understood the intimate connection between all of God's creatures, that we are all dependent on the creator for our very existence. Francis had a contemplative's sense of joy, wonder, and praise for each of God's gifts. Sean McDonagh points out: For Francis, every creature in the world was a mirror of God's presence and, if approached correctly, a step leading one to God.[4] Nowhere was this vision seen more clearly than in the Canticle of the Sun.

Francis had a kinship approach to creatures, a loving relationship with the elements of nature—both animate and inanimate. However, this was not always Francis' disposition toward the natural world. Thomas Murtagh points out that in the early stages of his conversion, the saint rejected earthly pleasures as a form of penance: "His appreciation of the worth of created things came only when he came close to God, and saw in creation a reflection of God's own goodness."[5] This appreciation led eventually to reverence. On Francis' attitude toward animals, for example, we learn:

On the surface (he was) a mere lover of animals; yet once one looks more deeply, one finds a respect, even a reverence for animals, and a presumption of basic equality. There is an expectation that animals also have moral duties. There is a personal charism that creates a bond with animals.[6]

Thus we see in Francis an evolution in attitude toward creation. Like us, he had to undergo conversion before he could relate to creatures in a familial way.

We could say that Francis had a "theology of inter-relationship" toward creation.[7] *In this theology creation has value because of its relationship to God rather than its usefulness for humanity.* "God looked at everything [that had been] made, and [God] was very pleased" (Genesis 1:31). The key word here is *everything*. The whole universe was created by a loving God who delights in what has been created. All creation belongs to a single community, everything is related.[8]

All creatures bless God. In the Canticle of Daniel (Daniel 3:52-90, *NAB*) wind and fire, ice and snow, mountains and hills, dolphins and birds, sun and moon, every living thing is called upon to praise God. In the canticle men and women are urged to praise God, but as Phil Land points out, "there is not the slightest suggestion that these bless God in a higher or even different fashion."[9]

Francis teaches us that we need to have a reverential attitude toward all of creation. According to Thomas Berry, we need to adopt a biocentric rather than a homocentric perspective toward nature.[10] This means that human beings should see themselves not as dominant over nature, but as beings who are part of nature. Thus, our focus should be on the living planet as a whole rather than simply upon humanity. In terms of spirituality, this involves an extension of the principle of the common good (from Catholic social teaching) to include all of creation. In this communal context, redemption has to do with more than the individual human being. We are all being saved together—humanity and the natural world (see Romans 8:18-22). Thus sin can no longer be considered as only personal; it is social and cosmic as well. The other side of sin is virtue. This involves, for the human being, appreciation for the giftedness of creation, compassion for its woundedness, and actions to advance the well-being of the planet.

Remembering Our Own Story

The grounding for an eco-spirituality comes from our own experience of nature. It is good to pause to reflect on the roots of our care for the environment and on the various stages of transformation that have brought us to our present level of appreciation.

Early in my life I had the opportunity to live on a ranch. The ranch belonged to my grandparents and was situated in northern California, about twenty miles north of San Francisco. I trace my love for animals back to this idyllic time of my youth. There were cows and chickens, a couple of horses, and a dog. My grandfather taught me how to milk a cow, a chore that took some getting used to as I kept squirting myself in the face with milk! Perhaps it was on the ranch that I first developed an ear for animal sounds, a gift which has given me an intimate rapport with various kinds of animals. This facility has also delighted a number of children as I bring to them the sounds of horses and cows, chickens and sheep, dogs and cats!

I notice an affinity with nature in the places I choose for retreat and for vacation—away from the city and its concrete dwellings and pavements, out to the countryside, to a farm, or up to the mountains. Even on my day off I prefer to be near a lake, some trees, a field, the beach, or in the stillness of the desert. Fortunately I live in San Diego where I am within an hour's drive of all of these.

In my retreat ministry I have been privileged to make a number of trips to Ireland. It is in this land of so many and varied glorious sights of nature—heather blossoming on a hillside in County Wicklow, the rugged landscape of Connemara, an ancient castle by the river in

Kilkenny, the many lakes and waterfalls that have a sense of timelessness about them—that my consciousness of nature's gifts has been profoundly deepened.

My friend Monica who lives with her husband and children in Dublin, Ireland, has an intuitive relationship with nature. She has helped me to experience a familial kinship with trees. One afternoon we were walking in a park that hugs the south side of Dublin. As we strolled along the path we shared our spiritual journeys with one another. Suddenly, Monica walked over to a large tree and put her arms around it. I was startled by this gesture and, hesitantly, asked her what she was doing. "I am drawing energy from the tree," she replied. I moved to where she was standing and asked her to explain this drawing of energy. She answered, "When you are in need of extra courage for some difficult task in life, go to a sturdy tree and, intuitively, draw the strength that you need, let the energy of the tree push you towards your task; when you are sad or experiencing anguish, draw forth from a tree the consolation and comfort that you need." I had always had a particular fascination for trees, sometimes even seeing them as symbols of myself, but finding a source of psychic energy in them was a revelation.[11]

As a result of my visits to Ireland, and the deepening sensitivity to the environment wherever I am, I now present retreats on spirituality and nature. I am indebted to Colm Lavelle, a Jesuit priest who has been directing nature-retreats in Ireland for many years, for his wisdom and prayerful respect for all that God has created. The following prayer exercise came from a conversation with Colm. It is an exercise I give to retreatants as I encourage them to walk in "God's garden" without analyzing what they are seeing. I suggest they do one activity at a time and contemplatively, not rushing to do them all.

A Walk in God's Garden

1. *Be there in the scene.* Lie on the ground, walk barefoot, hug a tree, stand in the rain, stand in the surf. See nature

as an icon: you have to see the icon before you can feel God's presence.

2. *Give thanks to God.* Pray a psalm from the Bible or let a psalm come forth from within you. Sing, dance, write a poem, whatever helps you to praise God.

3. *Be the object.* Be a tree, for example. Be a tree before God: listen to it, what are you saying to God? What is God saying to you? Or be a rock, a flower, the earth, etc.

4. *Explore the object as a symbol,* for example: a mountain, the ocean, a river, a blade of grass, an ant, a bird, etc. What is it saying to you about yourself? about God? about life?

5. *Transcend the object altogether and simply be in God's presence.* Utilize your five senses: look, listen, smell, taste, touch, but do not analyze.

Many of these prayer exercises can be done inside as well as outside. If it is a stormy day outside, or if illness prohibits your going out, choose a room inside your house where you can rest undisturbed in the quiet. Reflectively consider the things in the room that are made from natural materials, like wood, and apply the exercises that are appropriate. If you have indoor plants, make them the instruments of your prayer too. This form of prayer reminds us of St. Francis of Assisi for whom, "every creature in the world was a mirror of God's presence."

What Is a Disciple to Do?

In light of the extent of eco-destruction that now exists and of the insights we have received from such people as Sean McDonagh and Thomas Berry, it is the theology of interrelationship that will help creation. Inter-relationship implies interdependence. Like St. Paul's analogy of the body and Christ (1 Corinthians 12:12-26), each part of creation is dependent on the other for the smooth functioning and harmony of the whole. Nature is our own cosmic continuation, humanity's own extended self; to pollute it is to disfigure ourselves. Interdependence is the way to compassion for when one member of the body suffers, all the members suffer with it. I suffer with the earth, with the air, with the forests, with the water, when they are mistreated because they are part of my extended family. Compassion leads to justice. Indeed, compassion is the interiorization of justice. Compassion is the motivating force that drives us on to do justice spontaneously, willingly, and perseveringly. Two general responses are called for by the disciple: prayer and action.

Prayer

In order to be true citizens of the earth, we need to become attuned to the sins against nature as well as to those against people. "The earth is in agony," writes Al Fritsch, "it is covered by all the aspects of the crucifixion, the wounds of clear-cut land, the lance marks of stripped land, the thorns of litter."[12] We need to bring this expanded sense of sin to God in our prayers of petition. In addition, it is usually those who are economically poor who suffer the effects of cosmic sin the most. They are the ones, for example, who are most likely to have a toxic waste dump near their home.

One afternoon, after celebrating Mass at the mission church in Tijuana, I sat on a nearby hillside that overlooked a dry and dusty canyon neighborhood. As I prayerfully considered the scene before me, the words of Jesus on the cross came to me: "I thirst." I picked up pen and pad and jotted down these reflections.

My eyes settle on a steady stream
of dirty water, sewer water,
as it winds its way down the canyon.

Close by children ride their bicycles.
A boy stops to inspect some trinket
he spies on the dirt road.

A lone duck splashes in the urine-infested stream
hoping to cleanse its many feathers,
but instead brings germs to a nearby family.

Large bricks, rocks, and a few tires
hold down the roofs of some houses,
keeping those within free from the wind.

I can see the water truck
as it makes its way down the unpaved hillside
     road,
a perilous journey as it is traveling in reverse.

Children, in bright colored clothing,
wind their way through the few bushes and trees
and climb a "garbage-fall" in a spirit of adventure.

Many things of nature are in the canyon—
earth and water, brush and trees,
but they are in short supply
and everything I see is arid-dry.

In the expanded consciousness of the theology of interrelationship our prayer is at times explicit as we become aware of some devastation to nature or as we sing out our praise to God for the glories of creation. At other times when we do not know how to pray, "the Spirit also comes to help us, weak as we are ... the Spirit ... pleads with God for us in groans that words cannot express" (Romans 8:26). However, we live in hope, for we know "that creation itself [will] one day be set free from its slavery to decay and [will] share the glorious freedom of the children of God" (Romans 8:21).

Action

As we consider what efforts to make on behalf of the environment, it is well to keep in mind the basic norm proposed by Thomas Berry for enhancing the natural world and its functioning: *the well-being and integrity of the total earth community.*[13] The *Rerum Novarum* Conference, held to commemorate the 100th anniversary of the first social encyclical, presented five principles from which our actions must emerge: Focus on human dignity must be expanded to include the dignity of all creation, living and non-living; the option for the poor must include an "op-

pressed" earth; the common good is the good of all creation; the image of God is mirrored in the entire universe;
and global solidarity must be understood as solidarity
with *all* God's creatures.[14]

Al Fritsch, who has been an environmental activist for
many years, suggests seven viable models for action. Some
people fit better into one model's framework than another,
and many of us may take on more than one perspective at
a given time. Trust in the Spirit and consultation-in-com-
munity give us the confidence that we will discern and
choose what is best for our talents at any given time. Each
model possesses both strengths and weaknesses.

1. *The Caretaker Model*: Involves watchfulness, care, concern about creation stressing personal responsibility and
accountability.

Weakness: Lack of social analysis, that is, a lack of
attention to the underlying political and economic systems
and how social forces lead to environmental damage.

2. *The Partner or Creation-Centered Model*: Believes that we
have a relationship with Mother Earth; we learn from the
earth; we are to work in harmony with nature.

Weakness: Can be too philosophical/academic and too
light on the need for action.

3. *The Suffering Servant Model*: Sees the earth as wounded,
in need of humble service, engages in such efforts as
organic gardening, recycling waste materials, living more
simply; is willing to risk social standing or financial
resources for the sake of environmental action.

Weakness: Its non-political, passive character responds
at a local level, believing that when this local scene is made
right the greater whole will be helped.

4. *The Good Samaritan Model*: Sees the wounded condition
of plants and animals and takes an active and advocating
role in initiating the healing process; is aware of the inter-
connectedness of all beings.

Weakness: Practitioners of this model often work within

the system (analysts, researchers, performing environmental monitoring work, and so forth); may be too institutionalized or institutionally dependent, reluctant to confront the system that is wounding the environment.

5. *The Teacher Model*: Consists of environmental education professionals who develop educational materials or administer or teach in formal settings, as nature guides, etc. More active and critical of the system that has wounded the earth than models 3 and 4.

Weakness: Proponents often do not have the heart to take their activism to the streets or countrysides, but think it sufficient to describe or explain the current political, social, or economic situation.

6. *The Prophetic Model*: Sees the cosmic sin that threatens the integrity of creation and speaks publicly to the causes of environmental destruction, demanding social change; the prophet is willing to act alone, accepts nonconformity as part of the price, does not expect to be liked, respected, or applauded.

Weakness: The prophet may be short-tempered, overly-serious, self-righteous, harsh, dangerous, shrill, angry, and perhaps wrong. The prophet can become isolated from his/her base community of co-believers which community he/she needs for stability and strength.

7. *The Comic Model*: The serious nature of the environmental crisis places heavy stress on all who participate in the movement. A lighter tone, a chance to laugh at oneself, a bit of comic relief, and play, can do as much to save the earth as theological concern or prophetic thunder. This model complements all the others and enriches them.

Weakness: Comedy can be used against others in derision or sarcasm; comic material may be in bad taste.[15]

Final Thoughts

An argument against the theology of interrelationship which, as we saw, characterized the behavior of Francis of Assisi, is the proposed dualism of matter and spirit. According to this view, much of nature does not have rights because it is made up of dull matter. Jesuit paleontologist Teilhard de Chardin addressed this issue in his "law of complexity-consciousness."

> Everyone has known from the beginning that organized matter is endowed with spontaneity in combination with psychic inwardness. Everyone also knows today that this organic matter is amazingly complicated.... Absolutely inert and totally brute matter *does not exist.* Every element of the universe contains, at least to an infinitesimal degree, some germ of inwardness and spontaneity, that is to say of consciousness.[16]

This inwardness is known as the "within" of things. Sean McDonagh explains Teilhard's insight.

> From the first moment of the universe twenty billion years ago, every particle of matter carried within itself the seeds of everything that was to emerge in later unfoldings, including human consciousness.... According to Teilhard, the galaxies, the solar system, and the earth unfolded through a dramatic variety of sequences—from the initial energy in the "primeval atom," through the synthesization of matter in the first generation of stars, to the birth of life on planet earth, and finally to human consciousness itself. With the increased complexification of matter through successive transformations, there is a corresponding increase in interiorization.[17]

Interiorization, inwardness, the "within" of things: Teilhard conceived of reality as composed of both spirit and matter. This is what he called the psychic and physical components of things.[18] Matter is no longer seen as dead and inert. There is an immanence in the depths of matter. In *The Phenomenon of Man,* he wrote:

It is impossible to deny that, deep within ourselves, an "interior" appears at the heart of beings, as it were, seen through a rent. This is enough to ensure that, in one degree or another, this "interior" should obtrude itself as existing everywhere in nature from all time. Since the stuff of the universe has an inner aspect at one point of itself, there is necessarily a *double aspect to its structure*, that is to say in every region of space and time—in the same way, for instance, as it is granular: *coextensive with their Without, there is a Within to things.*[19]

Teilhard's insight saves humankind from the dualistic view of matter and spirit by stressing the fundamental unity of life in its inwardness, giving us a cosmic sensibility in the interrelatedness of all creation. Here is an excerpt from his potent "Hymn to Matter," an ecological form of prayer.

I bless you matter and you I acclaim; not as the pontiffs of science or the moralizing preachers depict you, debased, disfigured—a mass of brute forces and base appetites—but as you reveal yourself to me today, in your totality and your true nature.

You I acclaim as the inexhaustible potentiality for existence and transformation wherein the predestined substance germinates and grows.

I acclaim you as the universal power which brings together and unites, through which the multitudinous monads are bound together and in which they all converge on the way of the spirit.

I acclaim you as the melodious fountain of water whence spring the souls of men and women and as the limpid crystal whereof is fashioned the new Jerusalem.

I acclaim you as the divine milieu, charged with creative power, as the ocean stirred by the Spirit, as the clay molded and infused with life by the incarnate Word.[20]

As Sean McDonagh points out, we need to develop an eco-spirituality to counteract eco-destruction. In other words, we have to undergo conversion of the mind as well as of the heart. A basic transformation is needed in our way of viewing the natural world: from the belief that it is our right to conquer the earth to a sensitive caring for creation; from a dualistic view of matter and spirit to the fundamental unity of life. May the vision of Chief Seattle, a Native American of the Duwamish tribe of the state of Washington, be ours as well:

> Every part of this earth is sacred to my people. Every shining pine needle, every sandy shore, every mist in the dark woods, every meadow, every humming insect. All are holy in the memory and experience of my people.
>
> The rivers are our brothers. They quench our thirst. They carry our canoes and feed our children. So you must give the rivers the kindness you would give any brother.
>
> Remember that the air is precious to us, that the air shares its spirit with all the life it supports. The wind that gave our grandfather his first breath also receives his last sigh. The wind also gives our children the spirit of life.
>
> Will you teach your children what we have taught our children, that the earth is our mother? What befalls the earth befalls all the sons and daughters of the earth.
>
> This we know: the earth does not belong to us, we belong to the earth. All things are connected like the blood that unites us all. We did not weave the web of life, we are merely a strand in it. Whatever we do to the web, we do to ourselves.
>
> One thing we know: our God is also your God. The earth is precious to God and to harm the earth is to heap contempt on its creator.[21]

Nine

The Journey of the True Self

Get rid of your old self, which made you live as you used to—the old self that was being destroyed by its deceitful desires. Your hearts and minds must be made completely new, and you must put on the new self, which is created in God's likeness and reveals itself in the true life that is upright and holy.

—Ephesians 4:22-24

In chapter two we briefly considered Thomas Merton's notion of the true and false selves. Merton had many words to describe these two dimensions of the human person. He called the true self the real self, the deep transcendent self, the true "I"; and the false self illusory, incomplete, superficial.[1] Basically, the true self is that part of me that really believes I am loved unconditionally by God. It is the self God created me to become, the self in Christ grounded in the love of God. The false self is that part of me which wants to exist outside the reach of God's love, whether out of pride or despair. Inner freedom characterizes the true self, enslavement the false self. I am living from my true self when I desire what God desires; the false self however wants to go its own way either because of fear of what God may ask or because of an inclination to self-sufficiency.

Merton's quest for the true self came from two basic intuitions. The first intuition is: I am not what I ought to be; I am not what I appear to be. The self that I appear to be on the surface is not the real me, not the person I am in the depths of my being. The second basic intuition is: I can become what I ought to be. I can rid myself of all falseness, I can become free of the illusions that mask my true self and actually discover my true identity. I must go to God to find the real me. Merton wrote:

> The secret of my identity is hidden in the love and mercy of God.... Ultimately the only way I can be myself is to become identified with God in whom is hidden the reason and fulfillment of my existence.... Therefore there is only one problem on which all my existence, my peace and my happiness depend: to discover myself in discovering God. If I find God I will find myself and if I find my true self I will find God.[2]

A tension exists within each person striving to become his or her true self. St. Paul wrote of his own experience with this struggle:

> I do not understand what I do; for I don't do what I would like to do, but instead I do what I hate. Since what I do is what I don't want to do, this shows that I agree that the Law is right. So I am not really the one who does this thing; rather it is the sin that lives in me.... Even though the desire to do good is in me, I am not able to do it.... My inner being delights in the law of God. But I see a different law at work in my body—a law that fights against the law which my mind approves of (Romans 7:15-23).

It is not I who do it, not my true self that is in charge here, Merton would say, but sin which resides in me, that is, my false self. Perhaps a story from my own life will shed further light on this inner battle.

I have written in previous chapters about my ministry in Tijuana, Mexico. In the first year of regular supply work at the little mission church, Nuestra Señora de la Esperanza (Our Lady of Hope), I did not know a lot of Spanish. I could pronounce the words correctly, but I wasn't fluent enough to ad lib, for example, in giving homilies. This was especially true when we arrived at Holy Week with all its services. However, there was a realization deep within me that God wanted me to be at this church, a conviction that was reinforced both by the people of the area and by the Bishop's office. So I began my ministry there with high hopes. Gradually I adjusted to celebrating Mass and hearing confessions in Spanish.

I was acting from my true self, grounded in the love of God. I began going to the church in September of that year. In October, one of the families asked to have their child baptized. I said yes, but panic gripped me. I had never celebrated a baptism in Spanish before! A little voice within me whispered, "You should not be working here, you do not know enough Spanish." Doubts flooded in and I began to question my original decision to serve at the parish—my false self emerged. I brought this dilemma to prayer and asked God for freedom from the fear I was experiencing. The day for the baptism arrived, I was there and I managed to get through it fine. I came back to being my true self. This dynamic of panic-doubt/peace-confidence recurred throughout the year, each time something new to accomplish came along: a wedding, the feast of Our Lady of Guadalupe, Christmas Eve, etc. And each time I brought my feelings of panic and doubt to God, who had called me to this ministry in the first place. Getting through Holy Week successfully, with its many parts, was the *coup de grâce* to the fears and doubts. I now feel at home at the mission and, for the most part, am acting from my true self.

It was Merton's belief that we are to work *with* God in the discovery of our true self. He wrote, "We are even called to share with God the work of *creating* the truth of our identity."[3] Working out one's identity, however, involves anguish and risk. We need to face, and embrace, our shadow—that part of us that we are not conscious of, that has both positive and negative aspects. We need to confront our fears and insecurities, our guilts and compulsions, our need to be in control. We have to deal with hurts from the past that are lodged in our memory. We cannot go through this process unless we are grounded in the certainty that God loves us and is with us on our journey. For the only way we can become our real self is through the death of the false self. Our incomplete self must die for the true self to rise. Thomas Merton conceived of death, not as the separation of body and soul, but as the final disappearance of the false self and the emergence of the true self.[4] God takes us on this voyage to the realization of the real self through our prayer and through life experiences. The death of the false self does not happen in a day. As James Finley eloquently points out, "Like the birth of a baby or the opening of a rose, the birth of the true self takes place in God's time."[5] Our disposition must be one of surrender and patience.

The search for one's true identity is, then, a journey, not an exterior one that involves a change of geography, but an interior journey that calls us to find our own center, our own inner truth.[6] We are invited by God to travel along many inner avenues in our search for the true self, which avenues depends on each individual's personality and history. In his book, *Fire in the Belly*, for example, Sam Keen writes about the "soulful quest": a pilgrimage into the depths of the self that a man must take if he is to discover his true masculinity.

> We leave the sunlit world of easy roles and prefabricated tokens of masculinity, penetrate the character armor, get beneath the personality, and plunge into the chaos and pain of the old "masculine" self. This isn't the fun part of the trip. It's spelunking in Plato's cave, feeling our way through the illusions we have mistaken for reality, crawling through the drain sewers where the forbidden "unmanly" feelings dwell, confronting the demons and dark shadows that have held us captive from their underground haunts. In this stage of the journey we must make use of the warrior's fierceness, courage, and aggression

to break through the rigidities of old structures of manhood.[7]

What Sam Keen writes of a man's search for himself, Kathleen Fischer chronicles as modern-day woman's quest for her true self. She is writing here on discernment.

> This injunction to know the self and act from the deepest levels of the self is common in discussions of discernment. However, recent literature on woman's psychological development indicates that it can present special problems for women. In *A New Approach to Women and Therapy*, Miriam Greenspan lists among the problems which most often bring women to therapy that (1) they doubt their own competence, and (2) they feel they have no sense of self at all.[8]

In my experience of giving retreats to women, I find they do not usually need to be warned of the dangers of selfishness and self-centeredness. Their lives are filled with actions for others. They tend to work too much, often to the exclusion of their own need to be nurtured and to rest. Psychologist Jean Baker Miller looks into the cause of women's struggle to live their true selves.

> Almost from the moment of birth, there has been instilled in us the inner notion that acting out of one's self is a dangerous, frightening, and evil thing. Although such actions are encouraged in men, and become very enhancing to men's sense of self, self-worth, and self-esteem—they have the reverse effect for many women: threatening one's sense of self and producing a sense of unworthiness, evil, danger—or, at the very least, a sense of conflict and unease....
>
> This built-in threat has been a powerful force preventing most women from being able to connect freely with the first basic element of being alive—acting out of one's self and one's desires as one sees

them at each moment. It then prevents us from being able to formulate, to know, and state our desires.[9]

The journey toward the true self for many women thus involves a conversion from mistrust of self to self-confidence. They need to learn that being authentically oneself is also being the person God wants them to be.[10]

Dying to the "old" self has its painful moments as both Sam Keen and Kathleen Fischer point out. However, there is resurrection too as we gradually awaken to the beauty and the freedom of the true self. We are slaves no longer to this particular aspect of our false self. Being our real self is an experience of the power flowing from the resurrection of Jesus (Philippians 3:10). Sometimes we enter the process with a spirit of adventure. Such is the case of Susie who is discovering herself in an unusual location. The following is an excerpt from a letter she wrote to two friends, Bo and Sita Lozoff.[11]

Dear Bo and Sita,

Well, it's been a year and I finally went to trial. I've been sentenced to life imprisonment (which is only twenty-five years here in Canada); however, I am eligible for parole after ten years. I thought the "wait" would never end, but it has and my heart is full of joy.... I feel as though I'm finally going somewhere.

Even so, my time in this small building has served a great purpose: I've seen a lot of faces come and go, I've learned a lot about myself and others. I've learned the meaning behind your phrase, "Inside out." Indeed, my soul has finally been set free from the barriers I had trapped myself within.

I am actually glad (although I'm sure some see me as "mad") for the time I've received. Society is giving me a gift I would never have given myself: A chance to find my true self. Not only that, but they are giving me time ... time. Society has always seemed to me to be a mad rush of tension. Now I have ten years to sit back and learn about what life is really all about. Each day my spirit becomes stronger as it reaches the heights found in becoming one with God ... Love ... the Universe.

Love and Peace,

Susie

To come to the realization of the true self, we have to cross a chasm within ourselves. It is an abyss, writes William Shannon, that separates us from ourselves, that is from our real self.[12] We cannot make this crossing on our own. Our true self is hidden in our depths and the secret of who we are to be is known only by God. Our real self, the true "I," sleeps silently in our depths, waiting to be awakened by the Holy Spirit.[13] If we are left-brain, rational people we will crave a "five-point plan" by which to arrive at the true self; if our disposition is one of timidity and shrinking from pain we will be looking for an easy path. Intuition plays a big role in the journey of the true self. James Finley writes:

> Asking how to realize the true self is much like facing a large field covered with snow that has not yet been walked on and asking, "Where is the path?" The answer is to walk across it and there will be a path. One cannot find out first how to realize the true self and then set out to reach the clearly visualized goal. Rather, one must walk on in faith and as one goes on, the goal appears.... It appears not in a revelation of a fact but a transformation of our hearts, in which, without knowing how, God transforms us into himself and we begin to realize obscurely yet deeply that our lives are hidden with Christ in God.[14]

Yet, we are not alone in this journey of discovery. We do have the grace of God. We have the support of friends.

We have our own inner strengths. We are able to move forward in hope. Here again is Finley's description:

> No longer drawing our identity and life from what lies behind us but stretching forward toward our goal, we find that faith and hope meet each other, embrace, and sustain us. They become the feet with which we walk across the void and with abandon fall into it, lost to all but God.[15]

To illustrate the journey of the true self I will share, as I have in other sections of the book, a portion of my personal story. As I do so, perhaps something of your own search will be revealed to you. My reflections have to do with my affection for and love of women. It is and has been a long walk with the Lord, filled with dying and rising experiences, with risk-taking and inner healing, in a search for integration and wholeness. My recollections begin long before I joined the Jesuits.

I began dating in the eighth grade. We had a very precocious class, as our teacher used to lament. She thought we were too young to be going out on dates. I remember the parties at friends' houses. My dad would drive my date and me to the party and, dutifully, return hours later to take us home. In high school, dependence on the good will of my father changed when I passed the driver's examination and, subsequently, purchased a car. Now I could squire my girlfriends around in style. I dated all through high school, once with two girls from the same school and at the same time! I have very pleasant memories from those days. Often on the morning following an evening out with a girfriend, my mother and I would visit. She would ask how the date went, what we did, what the girl was like. I loved sharing with her because she was really interested.

I left home to go to college, my first time away from the family for any significant period. In my sophomore year, I met a girl I was to go out with for over three years. There was more depth to our friendship than to the high school romances I had. She was a wonderful woman, the kind of person I wanted to marry. Her family lived close to the college; they became like a second family to me.

Soon after graduation from college, however, I felt unsettled within. There was an absence of meaning in my life, even though externally it looked like I was doing fine. I suggested to my woman friend that we take a break from one another for a while so I could sort things out. During the next two years I went through what I call my "prodigal time." I lived with two other guys in a lovely house in the foothills. My affective life was full. I met women from a variety of backgrounds, some were Catholics while others had no religion (a new experience for me). The parties at our house were known far and wide. We called our place Villa Bacchanalian, after the god Bacchus, the god of orgy and revelry! Fast cars, liquor, and sex were plentiful in those two years. My attendance at Mass took a beating at times. Needless to say, instead of filling the emptiness inside me this lifestyle further dissipated my spiritual energies.

Toward the end of this two-year sojourn, my two roommates moved, leaving me with a lot of quiet time for reflecting on my life. A friend of the family had given me *The Imitation of Christ* for a graduation gift. I found it one day while I was rummaging through my belongings. I began to read it. I returned to regular attendance at Mass. Then one day while I was sitting in my office (I was a salesman for a food cannery), this thought came to me: "I think I want to be a priest." I was startled and frightened by this idea. The words seemed to come out of nowhere. When I asked myself what kind of priest, the answer was clear: a Jesuit. I had been taught by the Jesuits in both high school and college and so I knew something about them, but the idea of being one had never entered my mind before. One month later I entered the Jesuit novitiate at Los Gatos, California.

In the beginning of the Jesuit novitiate the novices make what is known as the "long retreat." This is a thirty-day experience of the Spiritual Exercises of St. Ignatius of

Loyola, the founder of the Jesuits.[16] In the First Week of the Exercises, one makes a review of one's life in light of God's love and mercy. In my recollections I saw clearly the sins of my past, especially those in the sexual arena. Guilt flooded into my consciousness. I deeply repented of past mistakes. However, in my newly found zealousness to follow the Lord, and a desire to be "perfect," I went overboard in my reaction to my past life. Out of fear of making a mistake, I closed off completely my feelings for women. I remained in this state of darkness for six years! During that time, if I saw an attractive woman I would immediately avert my eyes. I would not enter into friendship with a woman. I would be someone's counselor or spiritual director, but friendship was out of the question, so deep was the fear and the self-doubt. I am three-quarters Italian by descent, a lover by nature; those six years were an experience of living out of my false self as regards women.

While in theology studies, before ordination, I shared my realization of this repressed part of my psyche with a wise spiritual director.[17] He suggested an unusual prayer exercise, which was to put me on the path to my true-affectionate-self (a journey which I am still on, thank God). I was living in Berkeley, California at that time. Our house was close to the University of California. My spiritual director advised me to go to the university campus, find a place to sit where the students gathered, and deliberately look at the co-eds as they walked by. This was what St. Ignatius called an *agere contra* experience, that is, going against one's nature in order to achieve balance. Since my nature at the time was a repressive one as regards women, this exercise was the perfect beginning remedy. There, on the campus, I began the necessary process of dying to the incomplete self—for me, the fear of making a mistake, or the fear of returning to the lifestyle I had before joining the Jesuits.

It was not until a year after ordination that I felt sufficiently confident to become friends with a woman, ten years since I had joined the Jesuits. Not only did this woman and I share similar values, but she was physically beautiful as well, which warmed my Italian heart! I see God's hand in the timing of my reawakening and in the quality of the women who became a part of my life.

For the next ten years my relationships with women could be characterized by, "two steps forward, one back." Becoming one's true self takes time and I was, after all, also fully engaged in ministry during these years. I had to risk doing simple things: going to a movie alone with a woman friend, dining out in a restaurant together, visiting her parents, even signing "love" at the end of a letter to a woman friend, because each of these activities reminded me of the life I lived before joining the Jesuits. Then there were simple acts of affection—holding a woman's hand, hugging in more than a formal fashion, giving someone a kiss. Here again my desire for wholeness and the fear of it engaged in a kind of weird "dance," but with God's grace I kept moving forward. I continued to walk on the "large field covered with snow," making my own path. I was fortunate to have good spiritual guides along the way, mostly brother Jesuits who were integrated in this dimension of what it means to be truly human.

I meditated on Jesus' life and reflected on the ease with which he related to women. The very fact that there were women in his company (Luke 8:1-3) indicates that he was comfortable in their presence; women trusted him with their problems and their secrets, for example, the Canaanite woman who came to him to seek help for her ailing daughter (Matthew 15:21-28) and the Samaritan woman at the well (John 4:1-42); he was good friends with Mary and Martha, Lazarus' sisters. It is the story of the penitent woman, however, that most clearly speaks to me of his "at home-ness" with his sexuality. We recall the scene:

A Pharisee invited Jesus to have dinner with him, and Jesus went to his house and sat down to eat. In that town was a woman who lived a sinful life.

She heard that Jesus was eating in the Pharisee's house, so she brought an alabaster jar full of perfume and stood behind Jesus, by his feet, crying and wetting his feet with her tears. Then she dried his feet with her hair, kissed them, and poured the perfume on them (Luke 7:36-38).

Jesus does not push the woman away out of fear or embarrassment. He lets her wash his feet and then publicly forgives her sins. He is free and thus is able to affirm both her action and her faith. He is a model for me of integration and wholeness.

During a particularly graced and memorable retreat in the mid-1980s, I had a prayer experience that healed many memories and freed me from the effects of a pre-Vatican II emphasis on the evils of the flesh and suspicion of human desires and pleasures that made many of us feel guilty about our bodies and their urgings. I awakened one morning on the retreat with a deep sense of peace. Images came to me of a woman's body. As each image came to my consciousness, I found myself saying, "the beauty of the human body." Then images of my own body appeared. Again, I said the words, "the beauty of the human body," as each image came to mind. I felt deeply the truth of the beauty of the human body, male and female. There was no sign of the old fears, no feelings of guilt, just a deep-down peace. As the prayer diminished, I felt a great joy for this gift of love that had been given to me.

During the twenty-two years I have been a priest, I have met many wonderful women. Some have been in religious life, others married or single. I have faced and gone beyond numerous fears regarding my attraction toward women. Now, the depth of the friendships I enjoy is significantly greater than those of earlier years. I am amazed that these relationships pose no threat to my vow of chastity nor to my vocation. When I joined the Jesuits, it was beyond my comprehension that I would ever again have a woman for a close friend or allow myself to feel sexually attracted to a woman. I have benefited from the wisdom of others in this quest to be my true affective self. In particular, I want to mention two writers on spirituality and sexuality: Ben Kimmerling, a married woman from Ireland, and Patricia Livingston of the United States.[18]

I have developed a high regard for open communication with women friends so as to avoid misunderstandings or to uncover false assumptions about our relationship. Women friends tell me that this kind of sharing is very helpful for them as well.

The freedom I now have in my true self toward women has impacted all of my relationships. I am a more loving person to children, male friends, and the earth. The union I experience with God in prayer and throughout the day is testimony that I am on the right path to being more like Christ. In some ways I feel that I have come full circle except that now my center is Christ and the key reality is freedom, not license. T. S. Eliot puts the whole process into perspective.

> We shall not cease from exploration
> and the end of all our exploring
> will be to arrive where we started
> and know the place for the first time.[19]

The journey of the true self begins when we awaken to the unfathomable love of God for us. It is aided by such entreaties as the freedom-prayer for this method of communication with God enables us more spontaneously to accomplish what God wants. Our pilgrimage takes us down different avenues of prayer, as we have seen in this book—meditating on the scriptures, praying with our imagination, centering prayer, and the more quiet prayer of contemplation, to name a few. All the while we are striving to live a good Christian life, aware sometimes of the hidden presence of God who works silently in our depths. God leads us through various changes in consciousness—healing the wounds of the past, through the purifying dark night of sense and the terrifying dark night of the spirit, on to the intuitive non-dual experience and the ability to live more and more in the present moment. Christ-consciousness takes us out of ourselves as we feel more poignantly the pain of those who are suffering economic poverty and social injustice, and the wounds of Mother Earth. Lest we forget this two-fold dynamic of the spiritual journey, the inner and the outer, we have the words of Thomas Merton to keep us on track.

> One of the paradoxes of the mystical life is this: that a man or woman cannot enter into the deepest center of themselves and pass through that center into God, unless they are able to pass entirely out of themselves and empty themselves and give themselves to other people in the purity of a self-less love.[20]

I can think of no better way to conclude this book on the freedom to pray and the freedom to love than with the following Native American prayer, by an unknown author, and with a passage from St. Paul's letter to the Romans.

> Oh, Great Spirit, whose voice I hear in the winds
> Whose breath gives life to the world, hear me ...
> I come to you as one of your many children.
> I am small and weak.
> I need your strength and your wisdom.
> May I walk in the beauty.
> May my eyes ever behold the red and purple
>   sunset.
> Make my hands respect the things you have made.
> And my ears sharp to your voice.
> Make me wise so that I may know the things
> You have taught your children.
> The lessons you have written in every
>   leaf and rock.
> Make me strong.
> Not to be superior to my brothers and sisters,
>   but to
> Fight my greatest enemy, myself....

Make me ever ready to come to you with
Straight eyes, so that when life fades
As the fading sunset
My spirit may come to you without shame.[21]

Now that we have been put right with God
through faith, we have peace with God through
our Lord Jesus Christ. He has brought us by faith
into this experience of God's grace, in which we
now live. And so we boast of the hope we have of
sharing God's glory! We also boast of our troubles,
because we know that trouble produces endurance, endurance brings God's approval, and
[God's] approval creates hope. This hope does not
disappoint us, for God has poured ... love into our
hearts by means of the Holy Spirit, who is God's
gift to us (Romans 5:1-5).

Notes

Introduction

1. David Fleming, S.J., *The Spiritual Exercises of St. Ignatius: A Literal Translation and A Contemporary Reading* (St. Louis, Missouri: The Institute of Jesuit Sources, 1978), p. 23.

1. The Unconditional Love of God

1. Thomas Merton, *New Seeds of Contemplation* (New York: A New Directions Book, 1961), p. 75.

2. Gerard Fourez, S.J., *The Good News That Makes People Free* (Bethlehem, Pennsylvania: Catechetical Communications, 1976), p. 17.

3. Beatrice Bruteau, "Prayer and Identity," *Contemplative Review* (Fall, 1983), p. 2. This journal is now called *Living Prayer*.

4. Ram Dass and Paul Gorman, *How Can I Help?: Stories and Reflections on Service* (New York: Alfred A. Knopf, 1985), pp. 29-31. See also pages 194-196, on the "illusion of indispensability," in which we become so invested in our work that we actually begin to equate who we are with what we do.

5. Sr. Francis Brennan is a retired Incarnate Word Sister living in Houston, Texas. She is originally from Ireland.

6. Fourez, p. 18.

7. George Auger, C.S.V., "Forgiving and Loving Ourselves," *Human Development* (Winter, 1989), p. 40.

8. Quoted in Auger.

9. *Revelations of Divine Love: Julian of Norwich*, trans. by M.L. del Mastro (New York: Image Books, 1977), p. 124.

10. Edward Hays, *Prayers for the Domestic Church* (Easton, Kansas: Forest of Peace Books, 1979), p. 174.

11. *The Complete Works of St. Teresa of Jesus*, trans. and ed. by E. Allison Peers (New York: Sheed and Ward, 1946), Vol.2, p. 106.

12. Jean-Pierre de Caussade, *The Joy of Full Surrender*, revised trans. Hal M. Helms (Orleans, Massachusetts: Paraclete Press, 1986), p. 157.

13. Ibid., p. 156.

14. Thomas Keating, *Open Mind, Open Heart: The Contemplative Dimension of the Gospel* (Rockport, Massachusetts: Element Books, 1991), p. 76.

15. Merton, *New Seeds of Contemplation*, p. 16.

16. Wilkie Au, S.J., *By Way of the Heart: Toward a Holistic Christian Spirituality* (Mahwah, New Jersey: Paulist Press, 1989), pp. 27-28.

17. Kathleen Fischer, *Women at the Well: Feminist Perspectives on Spiritual Direction* (Mahwah, New Jersey: Paulist Press, 1988), p. 21.

18. Ibid., p. 116. There are various reflective exercises one can use toward enhancing one's self-image. Kathleen Fischer suggests some at the end of each chapter.

19. Fleming, p. 143.

20. J. Ed Sharpe, ed., *American Indian Prayers and Poetry* (Cherokee, North Carolina: Cherokee Publications, 1985). This prayer is by George Hunt, Kiowa Tribe.

21. Merton, *New Seeds of Contemplation*, p. 60.

2. A Prayer to Be Free

1. According to Thomas Merton, the false self is that part of us which wants to exist outside the reach of God's will and God's love. The true self, on the other hand, is the self in Christ grounded in the love of God. See *New Seeds of Contemplation*, especially chapters four, five, and six.

2. James Finley, *Merton's Palace of Nowhere: A Search for God through Awareness of the True Self* (Notre Dame, Indiana: Ave Maria Press, 1978), p. 97.

3. I have written elsewhere about this experience, "Facing Our Fears in the Call to Act Justly," *Spirituality Today* (Fall, 1985). See also my book, *Praying the Beatitudes: A Retreat on the Sermon on the Mount* (Dublin, Ireland: Veritas Publications, 1990), especially chapter six, "Blessed are the Single-Hearted." This book is distributed in the United States by Ignatius Press.

4. Finley, p. 117.

5. Beatrice Bruteau, "The Prayer of Faith," *Contemplative Review* (Fall, 1983), pp. 39 and 41. This publication is now known as *Living Prayer*.

6. Thomas Green, S.J., *When the Well Runs Dry: Prayer Beyond the Beginnings* (Notre Dame, Indiana: Ave Maria Press, 1979), p. 143.

7. Ibid., p. 144.

8. It is instructive to recall a description of conversion by Pedro

Arrupe, the late Superior General of the Society of Jesus: "Conversion is getting rid of something so that something else can take its place. It is getting rid of everything that prevents us from being filled with the Holy Spirit. Conversion, then, is a change; a change that takes place deep inside us, a radical change. Let us make no mistake about it, there is nothing superficial about conversion. It is not a giving away of something that we can well afford to lose. It goes much deeper than that. Conversion is a putting away of something that we *are*: our old self, with its all too human, all too worldly, prejudices, convictions, attitudes, values, ways of thinking and acting, habits which have become so much a part of us that it is agony even to think of parting with them, and yet which are precisely what prevents us from rightly interpreting the signs of the times, from seeing life steadily and seeing it whole."

9.   Dr. Beatrice Bruteau has two degrees in mathematics and a Ph.D. in philosophy. She has written books on Sri Aurobindo, Teilhard de Chardin, and her own approach to spirituality. She and her husband, Dr. James Somerville, are founders of Schola Contemplationis, a center for the study and practice of the contemplative life, especially the experiential realization of the interior goals of the spiritual life. They publish a Quarterly magazine-newsletter called *The Roll*. For further information, write: SCHOLA, 3425 Forest Lane, Pfafftown, North Carolina 27040. $10.00 per year.

10.   Beatrice Bruteau, "Prayer and Identity," p. 4.

11.   Ibid., p. 10.

12.   Ibid., p. 9. Also see her article, "The Living One: Transcendent Freedom Creates the Future," *Cistercian Studies* (Volume XVIII, 1983).

13.   Ibid., p. 10.

14.   Ibid., p. 15.

3. The Call to Contemplation

1.   Thelma Hall, R.C., *Too Deep for Words: Rediscovering Lectio Divina* (Mahwah, New Jersey: Paulist Press, 1988), p. 28. In this book the author offers five hundred different scripture texts organized under fifty themes, a valuable resource.

2.   Philip Sheldrake, S.J., *Images of Holiness* (Notre Dame, Indiana: Ave Marie Press, 1988), p. 110.

3.   Walter J. Burghardt, S.J., "Contemplation: A Long Loving Look at What's Real," *Praying* (March-April 1990), p. 10.

4.   John of the Cross, "The Ascent of Mount Carmel," *The Collected*

Works of St. John of the Cross, trans. by Kieran Kavanaugh, O.C.D. and Otilio Rodriguez, O.C.D. (Washington, D.C.: ICS Publications, Institute of Carmelite Studies, 1979), Book II, Chapter 13, Nos. 2, 3, and 4.

5. Teresa of Avila, *Interior Castle,* trans. and ed. E. Allison Peers (New York: Image Books, 1961), p. 66.

6. William Johnston, S.J., ed., *The Cloud of Unknowing* (New York: Image Books, 1973), p. 48, see also chapters four through seven.

7. Keating, p. 14.

8. Ibid., p. 35.

9. Ibid., p. 36. Thomas Keating writes further: "The meaning of the sacred word or its resonances should not be pursued. It's better to choose a word that does not stir up other associations in your mind or cause you to consider its particular emotional qualities. The sacred word is only a gesture, an expression of your intent....You should choose your word as a simple expression of that intent, not as a source of meaning or emotional attraction. The less the word means to you, the better off you are.", p. 49.

10. Ibid., p. 37.

11. Anthony de Mello, S.J., *Sadhana: A Way to God, Christian Exercises in Eastern Form* (New York: Image Books, 1984) explains this dynamic thusly: "Far too many people live too much *in their head*— they are mostly conscious of the thinking and fantasizing that is going on in their head and far too little conscious of the activity of their senses. As a result they rarely live in the present. They are almost always in the past or in the future. In the past, regretting past mistakes, feeling guilty about past sins, gloating over past achievements, resenting past injuries caused them by other people. Or in the future, dreading possible calamities and unpleasantness, anticipating future joys, dreaming of future events.", pp. 16-17.

12. Merton, *New Seeds of Contemplation*, pp. 222-223.

13. Keating, p. 46.

14. Ibid., p. 48.

15. Ibid., p. 49.

16. Thich Nhat Hanh, *A Guide to Walking Meditation* (Fellowship of Reconciliation, Box 271, Nyack, New York 10960; 1985).

17. Mike Rowland's music is available from: Sona Gaia Productions, 1845 N. Farwell Ave., Milwaukee, Wisconsin 53202. William Ackerman's from: Windham Hall Occasional, P.O. Box 9388, Stanford, California 94309. "Desert Dawn Song" is another calming recording and is available from: Soundings of the Planet, P.O. Box

43512, Tucson, Arizona 85733. The music of Taizé is very reflective. Although it has words, they are in chant style, a mantra set to music. These audio cassettes are available in many languages. In my retreat work, I often use the tape, "Laudate," which is in English and Latin. In my ministry in Mexico, I find the tape, Cantos de Taizé, an aid for reflecting with the people.

18. Merton, *New Seeds of Contemplation*, p. 80.

4. Putting on the Mind and Heart of Christ

1. Keating, p. 4.

2. M. Basil Pennington, OCSO, *Centered Living* (New York: Doubleday and Company, 1986), see pp. 82-103. See also chapter three, "A Mandalic Map of Consciousness," from the book *Eye to Eye: The Quest for the New Paradigm*, by Ken Wilber (New York: Doubleday Anmchor, 1983).

3. Bruteau, "Prayer and Identity."

4. "Eternity," in *William Blake: Complete Poems*, ed. by Alicia Ostriker (New York: Penguin Books, 1977), p. 153.

5. Keating, pp. 93-94.

6. I also practiced what authors Robert Bly (*Iron John*) and Sam Keen (*Fire in the Belly*) suggest as a way to heal father wounds: I grieved the loss of what my father did not give me. This, too, is a healing process. Here is a method for practicing the healing of memories prayer:

> 1. Relax in the presence of God who sees the past and wants to heal the effects of the memory in you. Ask God to help you see the past as God sees it.
>
> 2. Recall the painful memory or hurt that needs a healing touch. Let the memory surface. Take the least painful memory first; feel the feelings that the memory produces; tell God about your feelings and offer your hurt to God.
>
> Do one memory at a time and pace yourself in recalling additional memories, always choosing the least painful one next. You may need to wait a week or more before recalling the next memory.
>
> 3. Ask God to heal you with the kind of faith that *expects* results, believing that "nothing is impossible with God" (Luke 1:37, *NAB*); that "when you pray and ask for something, [believing] that you have received it ... you will be given whatever you asked for" (Mark 11:24); knowing that God loves you and wants you to be healed.

4. Thank God for the healing already happening within you. Pray for patience, the memory will be healed at God's pace.

7. Geoffrey B. Williams, S. J., "The Path of Contemplation," *Review for Religious* (November-December, 1988), p. 927.

8. Ken Wilber, *No Boundary: Eastern and Western Approaches to Personal Growth* (Boston, Massachusetts: Shambhala Publications, 1979), p. 62. See all of chapter five, "The No-Boundary Moment," for a thorough description of the present moment.

9. Bede Griffiths explains unity consciousness in the following way: "The self is not the little conscious ego, constructing its logical systems and building its rational world. The self plunges deep into the past of humanity and of the whole creation. I bear within my mind, my memory in the deep sense, the whole world. The movement of atoms and molecules, which make up the cells of my body, are all registered in the passive intellect (the source of intuition). The formation of my body in the womb of my mother in all its stages is stored in my memory. Every impulse of love or hate, of fear or anger, of pleasure or pain, has left its mark on my mind. Nor am I limited to the experience of my own body and feelings. I am physically and psychologically linked with all the world around me. My body is the focus of electro-magnetic phenomena, of forces of gravitation and all kinds of chemical changes. My feelings are reactions to a whole world of feelings both past and present in which I am involved. My mind is an unfathomable mystery, reflecting the whole world, and making me a center of consciousness among innumerable other such centers, each reflecting all." *The Marriage of East and West* (Springfield, Illinois: Templegate Publishers, 1982), pp. 155-156.

10. Bernadette Roberts, *The Experience of No-Self* (Boston, Massachusetts: Shambhala, 1984), p. 85.

11. Ibid., p. 89.

12. Ibid., pp. 89-90.

13. See chapter two of this book for a fuller explanation of creative freedom.

14. Roberts, p. 88. See also T. S. Eliot, *Four Quartets* (New York: A Harvest Book, Harcourt Brace Jovanovitch Inc., 1943), pp. 28-29, who describes this process in his own profound way.

15. William Johnston, S.J., *Silent Music: The Science of Meditation* (San Francisco, California: Harper and Row, 1976), p. 132. The chapter is called, "Cosmic Healing."

16. Ibid., p. 136. On the mystical life and mysticism, Harvey Egan

writes: "The word *mystica* came into Christianity by way of the famous late fifth-century Syrian monk, Pseudo-Dionysius, who wrote the mystical classic, *Mystica Theologia*. For him, mysticism involved the secrecy of the mind or that trans-conceptual state of consciousness which experiences God as ray of divine Darkness. Although the word mysticism is not found in Scripture, the Greek New Testament word *mysterion* is used to signify what many today consider mysticism to involve: the hidden presence of God and Christ in Scripture, the sacraments, and the events of daily life.... Perhaps mysticism can be tentatively defined as the universal thrust of the human spirit for experiential union with the Absolute and the theory of that union. More and more writers see religious mysticism as the intensification and full flowering of authentic religious living. An increasing number, too, emphasize that all genuine mysticism, be it Christian or non-Christian ... is actually authentic human living." *What are They Saying About Mysticism?* (Ramsey, New Jersey: Paulist Press, 1982), pp. 2-3.

17. Ken Eckel is a Catholic layman, retired, husband, father of five. He writes poetry in relation to his spiritual journey. He and his wife, Margaret, reside in San Diego, California. Unpublished poem.

5. Intuition and Prayer

1. Thomas R. Blakeslee, *The Right Brain* (Garden City, New York: Anchor Press, 1980), p. 6.

2. Ibid., p. 25.

3. William Johnston, S.J., *The Mirror Mind: Spirituality and Transformation* (San Francisco, California: Harper and Row, 1981), p. 78.

4. Quoted in Blakeslee, p. 48.

5. Quoted in Dass and Gorman, p. 94.

6. Griffiths, p. 169. Formerly a monk of Prinknash Abbey and Prior of Farnborough Abbey in England, Bede Griffiths went to India in 1955 and assisted in the foundation of Kurisumala Ashram, a monastery of the Syrian rite in Kerala. In 1968 he came with two monks from Kurisumala to Saccidananda Ashram, Shantivanam ("The Forest of Peace"), in Tamil Nadu. This ashram was founded in 1950 by two Frenchmen, Jules Monchanin and Henri Le Saux (who later took the Indian name, Abhishiktananda, meaning, "Joy of the Anointed"), and was a pioneer attempt in India to found a Christian community following the customs of a Hindu ashram and adapting itself to Hindu ways of life and thought. It is now a prayer center, where people of different religious traditions meet together in an atmosphere of prayer and grow together toward that unity in truth which is the goal of all religion. Bede Griffiths died May 13, 1993.

7. Frances E. Vaughan, *Awakening Intuition* (Garden City, New York: Anchor Books, 1979), p. 3. This book is a masterful work on intuition. The author guides the reader to a greater realization of his or her intuitive powers through specific exercises, which are combined with an examination of the role of intuition in such processes as dream analysis, creativity, and practical problem solving.

8. Ibid., p. 4.

9. Keating, p. 30.

10. Vaughan, pp. 9-10. Anthony de Mello, S.J., gives some excellent spiritual exercises for awakening one's intuitive faculty, drawing from both Eastern and Western traditions, in his book, *Sadhana*.

11. Blakeslee, p. 31. A fine introduction to dream analysis can be found in Ann Faraday's book, *The Dream Game* (New York: Harper and Row, 1974).

12. Griffiths, p. 165.

13. Vaughan, p. 4.

14. Griffiths, p. 155.

15. Ibid., p. 89. Section four of chapter two is on the doctrine of non-duality and is an excellent summary of this phenomena.

16. Beatrice Bruteau, "In the Cave of the Heart: Silence and Realization," *New Blackfriars* (July-August, 1984), p. 308. A reprint of this article and other articles by Dr. Bruteau are available from: SCHOLA, 3425 Forest Lane, Pfafftown, North Carolina, 27040.

17. Griffiths, pp. 90-91.

18. Ibid., p. 91.

19. Bruteau, "In the Cave of the Heart: Silence and Realization," p. 310.

20. Ibid., p. 311.

21. Galatians 2:20. The text as it is in the *Good News Bible* reads, "... it is no longer I who live, but it is Christ who lives in me."

22. Merton, *New Seeds of Contemplation*, pp. 281-282.

23. Griffiths, *The Marriage of East and West*, p. 93.

24. Pierre Teilhard de Chardin, S.J., *The Divine Milieu* (New York: Harper and Row, 1960), p. 116.

25. Ibid., p. 118, italics added.

26. Abhishiktananda, *Prayer* (London, England: S.P.C.K., first published in 1967, revised in 1972 and 1975, reprinted 1979), p. 54.

27. Bruteau, "In the Cave of the Heart: Silence and Realization," pp. 305-306.

28. Abhishiktananda, p. 24.

29. Bruteau, "In the Cave of the Heart: Silence and Realization," p. 314. Dr. Bruteau uses the term, "the self-realized person" to describe this reality. She writes: "The self-realized person has the mind of a child—unself-conscious, spontaneous, utterly pure in its sincerity and genuineness, in immediate and honest contact with the realities it meets, unblocked and uncomplicated, free and fluid, possessing a sense for the right, the true, and the harmonious.", p. 315.

30. Keating, p. 63.

6. The Dark Nights

1. St. John of the Cross, *The Collected Works of St. John of the Cross.* The major works of John of the Cross are: "The Ascent of Mount Carmel," "The Dark Night," "The Spiritual Canticle," and "The Living Flame of Love." Also in the *Collected Works of St. John of the Cross* are his minor works, his poetry, and a short biographical sketch of the saint.

2. Constance Fitzgerald, O.C.D., "Impasse and Dark Night," in *Women's Spirituality*, ed. Joann Wolski Conn (Mahwah, New Jersey: Paulist Press, 1986), pp. 291-292.

3. Thomas Merton, "The Inner Experience: Infused Contemplation (V)," *Cistercian Studies* (1984), p. 78. This is the fifth in a series of articles from Thomas Merton's unpublished manuscript, "The Inner Experience," ed. by Patrick Hart.

4. Thomas H. Green, S.J., *When the Well Runs Dry* (Notre Dame, Indiana: Ave Maria Press, 1979), p. 132, Footnote No. 7.

5. Maria Edwards, R.S.M., "Depression or Dark Night?", *Contemplative Review* (Winter, 1985), p. 36. This publication is now called *Living Prayer*.

6. St. John of the Cross, "The Dark Night," Book II, Chapter II, No.1, p. 331.

7. Merton, "The Inner Experience: Infused Contemplation (V)," p. 78.

8. Fitzgerald, p. 292.

9. Ibid., p. 291.

10. Leonard Boase, S.J., *The Prayer of Faith* (Huntington, Indiana: Our Sunday Visitor, Inc., 1976), p. 87. See also pages 83-91.

11. Green, p. 120. Constance Fitzgerald has this to say regarding

the temptation of self-doubt when one is in the dark night: "... how much easier it would be to bear the darkness were one not conscious of one's failures and mistakes. The most confusing and damnable part of the dark night is the suspicion and fear that much of the darkness is of one's own making. Since dark night is a limit experience, and since it does expose human fragility, brokenness, neurotic dependence, and lack of integration, it is understandable that it undermines a person's self-esteem and activates anxious self-analysis.", pp. 296-297.

12. Fleming, p. 207. Spiritual desolation describes our interior life when we find ourselves enmeshed in a certain turmoil of spirit or feel ourselves weighed down by a heavy darkness or weight.

13. Ibid., p. 209. See also pages 211 and 213.

14. Fitzgerald, p. 296.

15. St. John of the Cross, "The Dark Night," Book I, Chapter IX, No. 2, p. 313.

16. Fitzgerald, p. 296.

17. Eckel, unpublished poem.

18. Edwards, p. 35.

19. Ibid., pp. 35-36. See also Gerald May, *Care of Mind, Care of Spirit* (New York: Harper and Row, 1982).

20. A rainbow is an important symbol in African cultures. It signifies life. For the African Catholic, the rainbow is a symbol of the resurrection of Jesus. However, my realization of the significance of the rainbow in Africa did not come to me until long after the day described in the text.

21. A good resource on discernment of spirits is Thomas Green's *Weeds Among the Wheat* (Notre Dame, Indiana: Ave Maria Press, 1984).

22. Merton, "The Inner Experience: Infused Contemplation (V)," p. 78.

7. The Call to Compassion and Justice

1. Merton, *New Seeds of Contemplation*, p. 80.

2. This increase in population of an oppressed people reminds us of present-day conditions in the Third World countries and of oppressed people in so-called First World nations. In South Africa the birth rate of Africans is much higher than that of the white population; in the United States there is a growing number of Hispanic peoples despite their poor living and working conditions.

3. "Preferential option for the poor" is a phrase that originated in a meeting of the Latin American Bishops, in Puebla, Mexico, in 1979. Two sentences from that meeting are especially significant: "Jesus' option for the poor was preferential without being exclusive, a partiality consciously chosen in order to mediate a universality.... Service of the poor is the privileged, non-exclusive means of our following Christ." It is an option out of love. Peter McVerry, S.J., explains the option in the following manner: "It is a commitment to make the cry of the poor the primary demand on one's life, one's time, resources, and energy. It is a commitment to make their plight the primary objective of one's ministry and service. This is not to say that one's ministry is *only* to the poor; no, the gospel calls us to preach the Good News to all. But it is to say that even in ministering to the non-poor in society the primary concern—and the test of the effectiveness of that ministry—is what effect it has on the lives of the poor in that society." "The Option for the Poor: What Does it Mean in Ireland, 1987?" *Religious Life Review, Supplement to Doctrine and Life* (September/October 1987), p. 234. This journal is published in Ireland.

4. Donald P. McNeill, Douglas A. Morrison, and Henri Nouwen, *Compassion: A Reflection on the Christian Life* (New York: Image Books, 1983), p. 18, italics added.

5. The biblical translation I was using at the time of this prayer experience was the *New American Bible*. It is the same translation used here.

6. McNeill, Morrison, and Nouwen, p. 4. The noted white South African, Beyers Naudé, expresses the same sentiment in this way: "If you talk about hunger, go and see where hunger is. If you talk about injustice, go and view that kind of injustice. If you talk about human dignity, go and see where human dignity is being violated. If you talk about racial prejudice, go and meet with the people who know themselves and experience themselves to be the victims of that prejudice. Unless you are willing to do that, you can never discover the full truth of the gospel." "To Love When Others Hate," An Interview with Beyers Naudé, *Sojourners* (February, 1988), p. 17.

7. Walter Burghardt recalls the definition of contemplation given by the contemplative Carmelite William McNamara: "a pure intuition of being, born of love. It is experiential awareness of reality and a way of entering into immediate communion with reality." Burghardt points out that contemplation does not always summon up delight, for the real includes "sin and war, poverty and race, illness and death."

8. In discussing what is meant by "God's Will" and how it influences the way we act toward others, Thomas Merton wrote: "God's Will is certainly found in anything that is required of us in order

that we may be united with one another in love. You can call this, if you like, the basic tenet of the natural law, which is that we should treat others as we would like them to treat us, that we should not do to another what we would not want another to do to us. In other words, the natural law is simply that we should recognize in every other human being the same nature, the same needs, the same rights, the same destiny as in ourselves.... Not to act as if I alone were a human being and every other human were an animal or a piece of furniture." *New Seeds of Contemplation*, p. 76.

9. McVerry, p. 235. This is a challenging and enlightening article. Though published in Ireland, the insights of the author are equally applicable in the United States. McVerry (and others) points out that the infirm in Jesus' time were ostracized because it was believed that their infirmity was a punishment from God for some sins they had committed. See John 9:2 for an example of this.

10. Ibid, p. 235.

11. Jean Vanier, "At the Heart of Compassion," a booklet published by Irish Messenger Publications, 37 Lower Leeson Street, Dublin 2, Ireland. Jean Vanier is the founder of "L'Arche," a movement which seeks to give dignified life to mentally handicapped people.

12. Vaughan, p. 4.

13. Griffiths, p. 169. Pages 150-171 are on intuitive wisdom. This is an excellent treatment of intuition.

14. Dass and Gorman, p. 94.

15. Thomas Merton, *The Way of Chuang Tzu* (New York: A New Directions Book, 1965), pp. 52-53.

16. Karen Jaenke, "AIDS Ministry," *Fellowship in Prayer* (October, 1988), p. 33.

17. Dass and Gorman, p. 188. Chapter seven, pages 184-216, is an excellent discussion of burnout.

18. See *The Silent Prophet*, by Gerard Pantin, C.S.Sp., especially the Introduction. Printed by Servol Printing Services, Port-of-Spain, Trinidad, West Indies, 1982. The book contains experiences in spirituality and community from the lives of a group of workers in the ghetto.

19. Dass and Gorman, p. 102.

20. Ibid., pp. 111-112.

21. See my article, "Developing a Christian Social Conscience," *Review for Religious* (July-August, 1983).

22. Dass and Gorman, pp. 174-175. Chapter six, pages 153-183, is an excellent treatment of social action.

23. Jaenke, p. 32.

24. See William Johnston's book, *The Inner Eye of Love: Mysticism and Religion* (San Francisco: Harper and Row, 1978), pp. 26-27. Johnston comments on Mother Teresa's kind of service: "This is mysticism—and not a watered-down version either.... It is a profoundly incarnational mysticism wherein the eye of love perceives Jesus in the broken bodies of the destitute poor" (page 27).

25. Vanier, p. 11.

8. Compassion for the Earth

1. Sean McDonagh, *To Care for the Earth: A Call to a New Theology* (Santa Fe, New Mexico: Bear and Company, 1987). In this context, see especially chapter twelve, "Spirituality and Mission."

2. *The Pope Speaks*, Vol. 35, No. 3 (May/June, 1990), p. 206.

3. Louis Vitale, O.F.M., *Caring for Creation, Our Christian Calling*, (a booklet published by Franciscan Communications, Los Angeles, California, 1990), p. 4.

4. McDonagh, p. 131.

5. Thomas Murtagh, O.F.M., "St. Francis and Ecology," *The Cord* (Vol. 39, No. 4, April, 1989), p. 100.

6. Ibid., p. 108.

7. Wesley Granberg-Michaelson, "Renewing the Whole Creation," *Sojourners* (February-March, 1990).

8. We see in the story of Noah that the covenant God established was with more than human beings (see Genesis 9:9, 10, 13, 16). Of special note is this sentence: "God said to Noah and his [children,] 'I am now making my covenant with you and with your descendants, and with all living beings ...'" (9:9, 10).

9. Phil Land, S.J., "Eco-Theology," *Center Concerns* (Spring, 1991), p. 13. Published by the Center of Concern, 3700 13th Street N.E., Washington, D.C. 20017.

10. See William Madges, "A New Vision of Ourselves and the Earth," *Praying* (May-June, 1990), pp. 7-8.

11. I have found the following resources helpful in better appreciating trees: "The God Tree: Exploring Your Relationship with God," in *Women at the Well*, by Kathleen Fischer, pp. 72-73. "Familiar Trees of North America," published by Alfred A. Knopf, New York, an Audubon Society Pocket Guide, available for both Western and Eastern regions. *Wandering: Notes and*

Sketches, by Hermann Hesse (London, England: Triad/Panther Books, Granada Publishing Ltd., 1985). This book is filled with poignant reflections on nature. *Tree Roots*, guided imagery on audio cassette, by Lura Jane Geiger and Adam Martin Geiger (Lura Media, P.O. Box 261668, San Diego, California 92196).

12. Al Fritsch, S.J., *Renew the Face of the Earth* (Chicago: Loyola University Press, 1987), p. 39. All of chapter two is worth reading on the subject of sin and the environment.

13. See Madges, p. 8.

14. Proceedings of the *Rerum Novarum* Conference, held in Chicago, June 24-28, 1990, *Origins*, May 16, 1991.

15. Al Fritsch, "Environmental Activist Models for the 1990s," *Alternatives* (Winter, 1989). The address for *Alternatives* is: P. O. Box 429, Ellenwood, Georgia 30049. Some other resources for action are: *Eco-Church: An Action Manual*, by Al Fritsch with Angela Iadavaia-Cox (available from ASPI Publications, Route 5, Box 423, Livingston, Kentucky 40445); *The Global Ecology Handbook: What You Can Do About the Environmental Crisis* (Boston: Beacon Press, 1990).

16. Pierre Teilhard de Chardin, *Let Me Explain*, texts selected and arranged by Jean-Pierre Demoulin (New York: Harper and Row, 1970), p. 42.

17. McDonagh, p. 79.

18. Mary Evelyn Tucker, *The Ecological Spirituality of Teilhard* (ANIMA Books, 1053 Wilson Avenue, Chambersberg, Pennsylvania 17210), Spring 1985, Teilhard Studies Number 13, p. 6.

19. Pierre Teilhard de Chardin, *The Phenomenon of Man* (New York: Harper Colophon Books, Harper and Row, 1959), p. 56. A prayer exercise that brings out the "within" of things can be found in Edward Farrell's book *Surprised by the Spirit* (Denville, New Jersey: Dimension Books, 1973), pp. 119-121. It's called "A Celtic Meditation."

20. Pierre Teilhard de Chardin, *Hymn of the Universe* (New York: Harper Torchbooks, Harper and Row, 1965), pp. 68-71.

21. The entire letter is in McDonagh, pp. 148-151. See also, *The Good Earth*, a beautiful presentation of Chief Seattle's letter with pictures of creation, published by Sacred Heart League, Walls, Mississippi 38686. In my retreats on spirituality and nature I use an audio cassette by Robert Gass called, "O Great Spirit," a traditional Native American chant (Credence Cassettes).

9. The Journey of the True Self

1.   I draw my reflections on the true self and the false self from three sources: *New Seeds of Contemplation* by Thomas Merton, *Merton's Palace of Nowhere: A Search for God through Awareness of the True Self* by James Finley, and an article by William Shannon entitled, "Thomas Merton and the Quest for Self-Identity" (The Merton Center of Rochester, 4095 East Avenue, Rochester, New York 14610).

2.   Merton, *New Seeds of Contemplation*, pp. 35-36.

3.   Ibid., p. 32.

4.   Shannon, p. 173.

5.   Finley, p. 116.

6.   Shannon, pp. 175-176.

7.   Sam Keen, *Fire in the Belly: On Being a Man* (New York: Bantam Books, 1991), pp. 127-128. Keen begins his book with the following statement:

> A man must go on a quest
> to discover the sacred fire
> in the sanctuary of his own belly
> to ignite the flame in his heart
> to fuel the blaze in the hearth
> to rekindle his ardor for the earth.

8.   Fischer, pp. 115-116.

9.   Jean Baker Miller, *Women Changing Therapy* (quoted by Fischer, p. 115).

10.   See Au, pp. 61-63, for some enlightening reflections on what psychologists call, "introjects," that is, the "shoulds" that other people, consciously or not, impose on our lives, keeping both men and women from realizing their own deepest wants.

11.   Bo Lozoff, *We're All Doing Time* (Prison-Ashram Project, Route 1, Box 201-N, Durham, North Carolina 27705), p. 27.

12.   Shannon, p. 176.

13.   Ibid., p. 180.

14.   Finley, p. 117.

15.   Ibid., p. 95.

16.   The *Spiritual Exercises* of St. Ignatius, a classic retreat manual in the tradition of the Catholic Church for the past four hundred years, sprang from the rich mystical experiences and the dynamic spiritual principles with which God gifted Ignatius.

17. Ken Wilber has some interesting reflections on the dynamic of repression:

> What Western psychology discovered is that as higher-order levels of consciousness *emerge* in development, they can *repress* the lower levels with results that range from mild to catastrophic. In order to take into account this process of dynamic repression, we simply use the Jungian terms "shadow" and "persona." The shadow is the personal unconscious, a series of "feeling-toned complexes." These complexes are images and concepts which become "contaminated" by the lower levels—in particular, the emotional-sexual—and thus are felt, for various reasons, to be threatening to the higher-order structure of the ego-mind. These complexes are thus split off from consciousness (they become shadow), a process which simultaneously distorts the self-concept (the ego), and thus leaves the individual with a false or inaccurate self-image (the persona). If the persona and shadow can be reunited, then the higher-order integration of the total ego can be established.

Eye to Eye: The Quest for the New Paradigm (Anchor Books, 1983), pp. 90-91. See also chapter six, "Sexuality in the Service of Life and Love," in Au.

18. Ben Kimmerling, "Sexual Love and the Love of God: A Spirituality of Sexuality," *Doctrine and Life* (A four part series, 1986). *Doctrine and Life* is published in Ireland by Dominican Publications, 42 Parnell Square, Dublin 1. Ben Kimmerling, "Friendship Between Women and Priests," *The Furrow* (October, 1990). This journal is also published in Ireland (St. Patrick's College, Maynooth, County Kildare). "Have You Been Intimate Lately," an interview of Patricia H. Livingston, lecturer and counselor on intimacy and sexuality, *U. S. Catholic* (March, 1991). She uses psychoanalyst Erik Erikson's description of intimacy—the flexible strength for being close to another.

19. Eliot, p. 59. The quote is from part five of "Little Gidding."

20. Merton, *New Seeds of Contemplation*, p. 64

21. From *Earth Prayers* edited by Elizabeth Roberts and Elias Amidon (San Francisco: Harper San Francisco, 1991), p. 188.